THE TERMINAL GENERATION

*The Apocalyptic Words of Christ
for Such a Time as This*

R.C. COURSON JR., TH.D.

authorHOUSE®

AuthorHouse™
1663 Liberty Drive
Bloomington, IN 47403
www.authorhouse.com
Phone: 1-800-839-8640

Scripture taken from the King James Version of the Bible.

Published by AuthorHouse   07/08/2014

ISBN: 978-1-4969-0662-5 (sc)
ISBN: 978-1-4969-0661-8 (e)

Library of Congress Control Number: 2014907337

CONTENTS

Acknowledgments ix

Preface xi

Part I   The Urgency of These
**   Last Days: Revelation Chapter 1** 1

  1. Blessed is he that reads and hears the words of this prophecy and keeps those things which are written therein; for the time is at hand. Revelation 1:3
  2. The Patmos Vision, be prepared to meet the Alpha and the Omega. Revelation 1:8
  3. The command to write. Revelation 1:19-20
  4. The Revelation of Jesus Christ introduced to the Terminal Generation. Revelation 1:1-20

Part II   The Letters to the Seven Churches: Revelation
**   Chapters 2 and 3** 21

  1. The letter to Ephesus. The church at the end of the Apostolic Age, the churches first love is forgotten. Revelation 2:1-7
  2. The letter to Smyrna. The church in great persecution. Revelation 2:8-11
  3. The letter to Pergamos. The church under imperial favour, assimilated and settled into the world. Revelation 2:12-17
  4. The letter to Thyatira. The triumph of Balaamism and Nicolaitianism, and a believing remnant. Revelation 2:18-29.
  5. The letter to Sardis. The church of the believing remnant. Revelation 3:1-6
  6. The letter to Philadelphia. A true church and a professing church. Revelation 3:7-13
  7. The letter to Laodicea. The church in the final stage of Apostasy. Revelation 3:14-19
  8. The place and mind of Christ at the end of the Church-Age. Revelation 3:20-22

Part III Things That Shall Be Hereafter: Revelation Chapters 4–5 . 49

1. A door is opened in Heaven, the door of the Rapture of the church. Revelation 4:1-3
2. The enthroned elders. Revelation 4:4-5
3. The four living angelic creatures around the throne of God. Revelation 4:6-8
4. The worship of the elders and living angelic creatures before the throne of God in Heaven. Revelation 4:9-11

Part IV The Seal Judgments: Revelation Chapter 6 65

1. The Lamb opens the first seal and the wrath of the Lamb invoked. Revelation 6:1
2. The first seal, a rider on a white horse goes forth to conquer. Revelation 6:2
3. The second seal, a rider on a red horse takes peace from the earth. Revelation 6:3-4
4. The third seal, a rider on a black horse brings famine on the earth. Revelation 6:5-6
5. The fourth seal, a ride on a pale horse brings death upon the earth. Revelation 6:7-8
6. The fifth seal, a martyred remnant cries out for justice. Revelation 6:9-11
7. The sixth seal, world-wide anarchy, chaos, and confusion. Revelation 6:12-17

Part V The Seal Judgments Resumed, the Seventh Seal, and the Trumpet Judgments: Revelation Chapters 8–9 81

1. Silence in Heaven. Revelation 8:1
2. The seven angels with seven trumpets prepare to sound. Revelation 8:2-6
3. The first trumpet judgment. Revelation 8:7
4. The second trumpet judgment. Revelation 8:8-9
5. The third trumpet judgment. Revelation 8:10-11
6. The fourth trumpet judgment, Woe, Woe, Woe! Revelation 8:12-13
7. The fifth trumpet judgment, the first Woe is demonic affliction. Revelation 9:1-12
8. The sixth trumpet judgment. Revelation 9:13-21
9. The Blood Red Lunar Moons, and Solar Eclipses in 2014 -2015 on the Hebrew Holy Days. What do they mean? The wonders and signs in the heavens, a final warning.

Part VI   A Little Book Is Opened in Heaven: Revelation Chapter 10 101

1. A mighty angel holds the little book; the title deed to the world. Revelation 10:1-7
2. The end is near, "Thou must prophesy". Revelation 10:8-11

Part VII   The Seven Personages: Revelation Chapters 12–13 113

1. The woman is the Nation of Israel. Revelation 12:1-2
2. The red dragon is Satan. Revelation 12:3-4
3. The Child is Jesus Christ. Revelation 12:5-6
4. The archangel is Michael. Revelation 12:7-12
5. Satan and Israel during the Tribulation time. Revelation 12:13-16
6. The Beast of the Sea is the Anti-Christ. Revelation 13:1-10
7. The Beast of the Earth is the False Prophet and his mark is 666. Revelation 13:11-18

Part VIII   The Seven Vial or Bowl Judgments: Revelation Chapters 15–16 137

1. The vision of the seven last plagues, the vials of God's wrath upon sin. Revelation 15:1-8
2. The first vial, grievous sores without cure upon sinful mankind. Revelation 16:1-2
3. The second vial, the salt sea turned to blood. Revelation 16:3
4. The third vial, the fresh water turned to blood. Revelation 16:4-7
5. The fourth vial, men scorched with solar heat. Revelation 16:8-9
6. The fifth vial, darkness upon the whole earth. Revelation 16:10-11
7. The sixth vial, the Euphrates River is dried up. Revelation 16:12-16
8. The seventh vial, a voice cries from Heaven; "It is done!" Revelation 16:17-21

Part IX   The Revelation of Jesus Christ for the Terminal Generation 189

1. Religious Babylon is judged and doomed. Revelation 17:1-18
2. Commercial Babylon is judged and doomed. Revelation 18:1-24
3. God's view of Babylon, the human view, and the angelic view. Revelation Ch.17-18

About the Author 193

Information about this Book 194

ACKNOWLEDGMENTS

I express my appreciation to my parents, Mr. and Mrs. Robert C. Courson, Sr., for a godly heritage and for raising their family in the nurture and admonition of the Lord throughout my childhood and beyond as they modeled Christ in our home. My parents served as constant guides; they encouraged me to do all things in life as unto the Lord and to study to show myself approved of God (Proverbs 22:6).

To my professors and mentors at Crossroads Bible College in Indianapolis, who never strayed from the call on their lives and ministry to prepare men and women to reach a multiethnic, multicultural society for Jesus Christ. I am thankful for their patience and determination to teach the inspired Word of God and their guidance in helping me discern the call of God on my life and founding the Last Call Crusade and as evangelist (Matthew 28:19–20).

To my professors at Andersonville Theological Seminary in Camilla, Georgia, for their dedication to God's Word and the many hours they spent preparing course materials with a verse-by-verse exegesis of Scripture and for their unwavering commitment to the plenary interpretation of the Bible in every course (1 Peter 1:25).

To the Meadows Church family of Heltonville, Indiana, that ministered and encouraged my wife, Linda, and I during my battle with cancer, surgery, chemo treatments, and recovery. I thank them for their prayers and patience as I transitioned from serving as an evangelist to a church pastor.

I extend a very special note of appreciation to Elder Don Tanksley and his wife, Gaytha, whose encouragement brought this book to publication (Hebrews 6:10).

Finally, to my wife, Linda, who has been a constant source of encouragement and steadfast devotion as I received the call of God to enter full-time ministry. I believe the call and road to ministry was more difficult for Linda, and I would not have completed my doctorate in theology without Linda guarding my private time of study and seclusion with the Word of God. My wife has been a godsend to me and many others during her forty years of service and ministry to others as a registered nurse (Proverbs 31:10–31).

PREFACE

Before you read this book, I encourage you to understand that we are the **terminal generation** according to the **empirical, scientific, and biblical evidence I will** present in this book. Simply put, our generation, *the baby boomers, the hippies, the yuppies, generation X, and the millennials,* will be alive when humanity's greatest cataclysmic event sounds in our life.

As you read this book, realize that the world and your life as you know it today are **about to change forever.** Jesus Christ is coming soon, suddenly, silently, to **rapture His church;** the **anti-Christ** will ascend to dominate world power; and the **wrath of God** will be unleashed on sinful people during the **great tribulation.** This book is an instruction manual covering the things to come in our life and a survival manual of protection and preparation; **be prepared, and don't be left behind!**

In the sixties and early seventies, a major shift in American society ushered in the terminal generation. This shift covered a gamut of political, social, economic, and moral issues; though many point their fingers at the war in Vietnam, the peace movement, the civil rights movement, the feminist movement, or the drug culture and acid rock, these were only symptoms of the disease.

Without a doubt, there was a shift in America's moral fabric, and we only now begin to realize the slippery slope we started down with the *Roe v. Wade* decision in 1973. The Supreme Court paved the way for abortion on demand in America, and its decision has resulted in the slaughter of 64 million innocents and the loss of the sanctity of life in America. Children now carry guns to school, students and teachers are murdered in schools, gangs participate in drive-by shootings in major cities and rural America alike. Our nation is caught up in the debate for a constitutional amendment on the sanctity of marriage between one man and one woman, same-sex marriages, and civil unions. President Thomas Jefferson asked, "What price will America pay for slavery?" The response from God for the oppression and brutality of slavery was the Civil War.

The questions for our generation are, What price will America pay for the abortion of the innocents? What price will America pay for its gross immorality as a nation? We will reap the wrath of God in this **terminal generation.**

What changed? There is one culpable, precipitating, and undeniable fact in the denigration of America that has led our nation to the precipice of disaster: the **gradualization of the church,** not the marginalization of our society. The bedrock foundation of American society and our moral fabric and fiber is the inerrant Word of God. The Bible stands as final authority in all matters of life, faith, and practice for a society. The Word of God is the all-encompassing guide for morality and ethnicity in all branches of our government, society, the family, and the home. The moment America began to shift from the Laws of God, His Commandments, ordinances, and judgments that are mirrored in our Constitution, our nation changed forever.

The change was gradual; prayer and the Bible were removed from schools, the nation became tolerant of sin and immorality in the name of social justice, and our nation embraced a worldview rather than God's view. Corporate and personal gain became the norm for our society spurred on by slogans such as "Get yours first," "Second place is the first loser," and "Those with the most toys when they die win."

When American parents no longer taught their children the Word of God, when His Word was no longer proclaimed from the pulpits, we lost our moral compass in our communities, schools, homes, and in the next generation of Americans. The silence of the Word of God in America is deafening. We have mortgaged our next generation for the sake of comfort rather than conviction and for compromise rather than consecration. We have become tolerant of sin and less tolerant of God's Word and guiding principles in Scripture. The result has been disastrous; the free world has been wounded. Galatians 6:7 instructs us, "Be not deceived: for God is not mocked. For whatsoever a man soweth, that shall he also reap" (KJV).

We have forgotten how to tell time in America; church pulpits have been silent for the last forty years concerning **eschatology and end-time events and failed to sound the two-minute warning.** In Ezekiel 22:30, the prophet Ezekiel recorded that God looked for a man in his generation to stand in the gap for Him, to sound out the warning as a watchman on the tower, but He could find none. Christianity in America is 2,500 miles wide but only inches deep; the gospel of Christ has been diluted; and the blood of the Lamb, sin, repentance, and holiness have been removed in favor of the warm platitudes of self-righteousness so we can all feel good about ourselves and free from any sense of responsibility to anyone but ourselves.

Today is the day of salvation (2 Corinthians 6:2; Isaiah 49:8). Not tomorrow, not next week, but today. This is apparent in the shift of American music in the late 1960s with a song by the rock band *Chicago that asked, "Does anyone know what time it is?"* The lyrics remain a fitting question for you as you read this book; what time is it today according to God's prophetic clock? Today, we stand at the crossroads of time and eternity, and the sands of time are sifting slowly and silently through the hourglass of our **terminal generation** almost without notice. This book is an alarm clock ringing out the warning that your life and the world as you know it are about to change forever.

The Bible reads like a road map through time past, present, and future. If you are skeptical of the Word of God, this book will erase your doubts and solidify your suspicions concerning current world events. My purpose in citing Scripture is not to offend or criticize you but to rouse your intellect to give serious consideration to the inspired Word of God.

The Bible tells us that God is not the author of confusion; He desires us to know Him and His plan for the ages. The minor prophet Amos recorded for us in Amos 3:7, "Surely the Lord God will do nothing but he revealeth his secrets unto his servants the prophets." God has given us prophecy to warn us, to prepare us, and to remove our fears and doubts of the unseen things and events that will shortly come to pass.

The Bible tells us that God is not slack concerning His promises to us and is not willing that any should perish; He wants all to repent (2 Peter 3:9). God has foretold the events concerning the last days, and His words confirm that His greatest desire for our lives is salvation, not separation (John 3:16–17). God promised eternal life to the righteous and judgment and eternal damnation of the unrighteous (John 3:36; 1 John 5:12–13).

I encourage you to understand that we are the **terminal generation,** and from the beginning, I want to make it clear that it is vitally important that this book be true to Scripture. I believe that my writings and conclusions, even those that depart significantly from current evangelical thinking, will stand up to biblical scrutiny. Compare Scripture reference to Scripture reference (2 Peter 1:19–21), know that no passage of Scripture admits of private interpretation, test everything according to the inerrant Word of God (2 Timothy 3:16), and hold onto what is good (1 Thessalonians 5:21).

I call on readers to be like the Berean Christians, who examined the Scripture every day to see if those words were true (Acts 17:11).

PART I

THE URGENCY OF THESE LAST DAYS: REVELATION CHAPTER 1

Scripture Text: Revelation 1:1–4

The revelation of Jesus Christ as presented in the final book of the Bible is the revealing of God's plan for the ages; the book of Revelation is history, His story, and our road map through time since the creation of all things (Genesis 1:1).

The book of Revelation is singular, not plural as often misquoted; it is not the revelations of Jesus Christ but the revelation or revealing of Jesus Christ and His message of encouragement to the saint and a warning to a lost and dying world. Revelation provides an intimate look at the person, character, nature, and personality of Jesus Christ through His names, titles, deity, power, majesty, glory, deeds, and His role and rule as the King of Kings and Lord of Lords seated at the right hand of His Father (John 3:16–17).

Revelation is the only prophetic book in the New Testament, and its inspired prophecy reveals the divine, sovereign will of God to all humanity as this present age comes to a close. God has given us the book of Revelation in fulfillment of His promise to the prophet Amos in the Old Testament: "Surely the Lord God will do nothing but he revealeth his secrets unto his servants the prophets" (Amos 3:7).

Everything in Revelation will be fulfilled exactly according to the Scriptures in the fullness of time according to the Word of God. There is a one-word answer to the skeptic who does not believe the Bible is the inspired Word of God—prophecy! Clearly, 28 percent of the Bible is prophetic, and the perfect accuracy of the prophetic portions proves without question that the Bible is of divine origin. The teaching and instruction of Bible prophecy are of paramount importance for the churches today and this **terminal generation.** Nothing motivates Christians like the study of prophecy; it puts an evangelistic fire in the heart of the church, it gives believers a vision for world missions and injects in them a desire to live holy lives in an age of unholiness.

In this book, as much as possible in the context of each chapter, the *apocalyptic words of Christ* will be referenced to the New and Old Testament prophesies concerning Christ and the Old Testament prophets

Isaiah, Ezekiel, Jeremiah, Ezra, Nehemiah, Daniel, and the twelve minor prophets. This book will carry us from **Creation (Genesis 1:1) to re-creation (Revelation 21:5)** and will be a literal (plenary interpretation) of the Bible. The symbolic, allegorical, or metaphorical sections of Scripture will be defined by comparing Scripture with Scripture. An example of this is the stars and candlesticks in Revelation 1:20; they are interpreted and explained by Jesus Christ as the seven pastors and seven churches of Revelation 2 and 3.

Revelation opens with the primary subject of the book, Jesus Christ, and the recording author is introduced as John the apostle. John received a vision from God and a charge to write and record according to the words of Christ those things that are and will be.

The first three chapters introduce Jesus Christ, the incarnate Son of God; John, the beloved apostle of Christ; and the purpose of the letters to the seven churches. It is noteworthy that each church existed in the first century AD and symbolically represents a specific time in the **church age.** The church age began on the day of Pentecost (Acts 2:1–47) with the giving of the Holy Ghost to all believers as promised by Christ before His passion, resurrection, and ascension to heaven (John 16:7; Luke 24:49; Acts 1:8). The present age is often referred to as the age of the Gentiles, the church age, or simply the age of grace. The church age, speaking of the church specifically, will end at the **rapture of the church.** (The term used in Scripture is the Greek word *harpazo*, **"catching away."**) The rapture of the church will be covered and explained in fuller detail in the discussion of chapter 4 of Revelation, when the church was gathered unto Christ immediately prior to the tribulation period of three and a half years and the great tribulation period of three and a half years. This was a full seven years of 360 days, each based on the Jewish calendar to the exact date of prophecy as given in the writings of the prophet Daniel and the apostle John.

Thoughts as We Begin This Study and Begin to Examine the Evidence of The Terminal Generation

There are only seven letters to seven churches representing a historical period in the first century; they are symbolic of a specific historical period in the centuries that followed, up to and including our present generation in the age of the Laodicean church.

The obvious conclusion from Scripture is revealed in the fact that there is no eighth letter; it was not lost or forgotten by God. Simply put, the church age will draw to a close with the apostasy and falling away from Christ and truth in the twenty-first-century church of the present age. (See 2 Thessalonians 2:3, 1 Timothy 4:1–2, 1 John 4:1–4, and Jude 1:19 for the condition of the church today. Compare those Scriptures with Romans 1:18–32 and 2 Timothy 3:1–7 for the conditions of the world today.)

When we compare these verses to the Olivet Discourse in Matthew 24 and 25, we can have little doubt that we are the **terminal generation of the church age.**

I have taught and preached Revelation in its entirety several times from the pulpit with the titles, **"Escape the Coming Darkness," "Flee to Jesus," and "The Approaching Hoofbeats,"** and in this book, I will simply title it **"Be Prepared"** for the terminal generation.

Revelation 1:1–4

The apostle John had been exiled to the rocky, barren island of Patmos, which is off the coast of Asia Minor. The island is ten miles long and six miles wide. John was exiled there by the Roman emperor Domitian in AD 95. Domitian was the brother of the Roman general Titus, who besieged the city of Jerusalem in AD 70. Upon entering the city, he destroyed the Jewish temple as prophesied by Christ in Matthew 24:2, Mark 13:2, and Luke 19:44, 21:6. It is interesting that God allowed one pagan brother to destroy the earthly temple in Jerusalem and another pagan brother, Emperor Domitian, to banish John to an island to be alone with Christ and write about the heavenly temple of God and the new Jerusalem.

The present tribulation and persecutions John recorded for us in Revelation 1:9 were founded in the anti-Christian and anti-Semitism of the Roman ruling class, the Caesars, and the Senate of Rome. Rome zealously persecuted the nation of Israel, the Christians, and the church from the days of Christ until the Edict of Toleration by Constantine in AD 313. There were four primary reasons given historically for the persecution of the Jewish nation, Christians, and the church.

1. The Romans worshipped many gods while the Jews and Christians worshipped the one true Living God, Jehovah, and Christians worshipped the incarnate and resurrected Son of God, Jesus Christ.

2. **The** Romans persecuted the Jews and Christians because they would not pay taxes or tribute or offer sacrifices to pagan gods.

3. Christians were persecuted because they modeled the life and teachings of Jesus Christ and abstained from immorality and brazen, ungodly lifestyles. Pagan Romans were convicted of their sins and iniquities because of the testimony of the church.

4. Rome sought the destruction of the early church and the genocide of all Christians, and it used the Christians as a scapegoat for the nation's civil unrest. This is much the same as the actions and accusations of Hitler and Nazi Germany against the Jews during World War II, the country's **"Final Solution" document, and** the death camps that resulted in the execution of 7 million Jews. Emperor Nero blamed Christians for the social problems of the Roman Empire and decreed that all Christians were to be killed. Historically, Nero was responsible for the burning of Rome, not the Christians.

Revelation was written between AD 95 and 100; the earlier date fits best with secular and Bible history. The apostle John was the last living apostle; he brought the apostolic age to a close.

Who were the apostles? They were those who saw the resurrected Christ, received commissions directly from Him, and had all the gifts of the Holy Spirit, including *healing, miracles, tongues, and the interpretation of tongues.* In addition, they received the continuing gifts of the Spirit for ministry and the perfecting of the saints. (For further study of the apostles, research Luke 6:12–16, Matthew 10:2–4, Mark 3:13–19, Acts

1:15–26, Acts 9:1–16, 1 Corinthians 1:1, 2 Corinthians 1:1, Galatians 1:1, and Ephesians 4).

Revelation's theme, Jesus Christ, is presented in a threefold manner:

1. As to the time which is, was, and will come, encompassing the past, the present, and the future of humanity from Creation to re-creation.

2. As to Christ's relationship with His church (Matthew 16:18; Revelation 2–3), to His promised return for His church (John 14:1–6; Revelation 19), to His seal, trumpet, woe, and vial judgments of the tribulation time (Revelation 6–19), to His kingdom (Revelation 19–22), to His offices as prophet, which began at Christ's First Advent, to His office as priest, which began at His ascension to heaven and continues to this day interceding for sinners (1 John 2:1–2), His office as King of Kings and Lord of Lords (Revelation 19:16), and His relationship as the bridegroom to His bride, the church (Revelation 21:2, 9, 22:17).

3. As to Christ's Second Advent (distinct from the rapture of the church) and the establishment of His millennial kingdom on earth as given in Bible prophecy (Isaiah 9:6–7; Micah 5:2; Revelation 20:1–6). This will be discussed in detail later in this book and will refer to the prophecy of Daniel (12:11–13) dating the establishment of the millennial reign of Christ beginning exactly seventy-five days following the Second Advent of Christ at the end of the seven years of tribulation and the Battle of Armageddon.

We will see in this study several parenthetical passages and interludes in Revelation as well as typologies of Christ presented in the Old Testament that Jesus Christ fulfilled in the New Testament. The test of Abram to offer his son Isaac to God and the Passover Lamb of Exodus was fulfilled in Christ, the Lamb of God (Isaiah 53:1–8; John 1:29; Revelation 5:1–6). The interlude or intermission chapters of Revelation include the sealing of the 144,000 witnesses of the gospel from the twelve tribes of Jacob/Israel; the two witnesses who will stand before God and prophesy at the Western Wall in modern-day Jerusalem (Revelation 11); the Lamb, the remnant, and the everlasting gospel of (Revelation 14); the gathering of the kings at Armageddon (Revelation 16); and the four alleluias in heaven (Revelation 19).

The scene and setting of this book begins with John's vision on Patmos; throughout the remainder of the book, the scene shifts between earth and heaven. The scene changes will be called out according to the context of the chapter and Scripture passage.

Here are several important points.

1. Revelation is the only book in the Bible's sixty-six books that offers a blessing to those who read and hear these prophetic words of God.
2. Revelation ends with a stern warning: "Woe unto anyone who adds to or takes away from this book." For this reason, we must consider the perversion and corruption of the Bible today as publishers have deleted Scripture, changed the words of God, or added to the original inspired Word of God in the original language and properly translated in the King James Version. The further we get away from God's Word, the further we get from God.
3. Revelation is literal unless otherwise revealed in the context and content of the passage. God is not the author of confusion. Revelation is not a sealed book; the Lord has given it to us so we might order our lives according to the urgency of the hour in the distribution of the gospel to those without.
4. We will never get lost in Revelation as long as we remember that Jesus Christ is seated on the throne next to God the Father, as long as we remember who Jesus Christ is—the King of Kings and Lord of Lords, and as long as we remember what is happening in the context of the Scripture passages of Revelation.
5. We must remember that where the Bible is silent, we should also be silent. We don't know when the rapture will take place, but we know from Scripture that there remains no elements of Bible prophecy that must be fulfilled before Jesus Christ returns for His church. It may be today! We do not know what 666, the

mark of the beast, translates as, but we do know the timing of the mark and that it will appear on the right hands or foreheads of individuals. We know the eternal destiny of those who receive the mark of the beast; they will be doomed to the lake of fire, hell, forever. We do not know what the voice of the thunders cried, but we know when the voices will roar.

Be Prepared

Revelation opens with an introductory statement of biblical fact: "The Revelation of Jesus Christ which God gave unto him" (Revelation 1:1), and it sets the theme for the remainder of this prophetic book. In Revelation 1:9–10, God revealed to the apostle John through a divine vision the past, the present, and the future state of the world and Jesus Christ's Second Advent to establish His kingdom.

This study will view Revelation 1–3 in the prophetical sense of those historic elements of the church age in times past, and this was revealed to John in his visions in chapters 1–3. We will study the prophetic truths that are to be fulfilled in chapter 4 and following. These future events were revealed to John as his presence shifted to scenes of heaven. The Bible mentions three heavens. The apostle Paul mentioned in Corinthians 12:1–4 of being caught up either in the spirit or the flesh into the third heaven. The Word of God given in the Scriptures as defined in the original language of the Bible lists three heavens. The first heaven is our atmosphere, which provides our protective cover from the sun's rays, nourishes the earth with sunshine and rain, and supports the earth's weather patterns (Psalm 19:1–6). The second heaven as noted in the Bible is outer space, where millions upon millions of solar systems exist according to the creative will and design of God (Genesis 1:1; Job 38:31–33; Psalm 19:1–6). The third heaven mentioned in the Bible is God's abode or dwelling place, which will be covered in great detail in our study of Revelation 5, 10, 19:1–10, and 21–22.

To aid in the reading, study, and understanding of this book and study guide of end-times prophecy, a verse-by-verse exegesis/interpretation will be given that will follow a general verse-by-verse format and explanation.

It would be most helpful to have your Bible opened to the passages of Scripture referenced as you read and study. Please write down your notes, thoughts, or questions as you read. I may be contacted through my email address robertcoursen@sbcglobal.net

Chapter One Outline

1) Introduction to Revelation
   a) The method of delivery—verse 1
   b) The record of the message—verse 2
   c) The blessing of the message—verse 3
   d) The urgency of the message—verse 4
   e) The span of the message—verse 19
2) The salutation of Revelation
   a) To the seven churches in verse 4 (There were more than seven first-century churches, but these seven have prophetic and historical significance in this church age prophecy we will study in the later chapters of Revelation.)
   b) The eternality of Jesus Christ—verse 4
   c) The names of Jesus Christ to authenticate Scripture as of divine origin—verses 5–8
3) The Patmos vision of the apostle John
   a) John on Patmos for the Word of God—verse 9
   b) John in the spirit—verse 10
   c) Jesus Christ spoke and commanded John to write—verse 11
   d) John saw Jesus Christ, the candlesticks, and the stars—verses 12–18
   e) Jesus Christ explained the vision to John—verses 19–20

The grand theme and subject of this prophetic book of the New Testament is introduced to us in verse 1; it is the person of Jesus Christ, the only begotten Son of God (John 3:16; Luke 3:21–22; Matthew 17:1–5). The Bible is **Christocentric, that is,** Jesus Christ is the primary subject of the Scriptures from the earliest announcement of the Father, Son, and Holy Spirit—the Trinity—at Creation (Genesis 1:26) and to the announcement of humanity's Redeemer in our first **messianic prophecy of the Bible,**

Genesis 3:15. Jesus Christ is the thin red line of blood woven throughout the Old and the New Testaments and concludes in Revelation 22:20, "Surely I come quickly."

The method of the messages' delivery was a vision and a message from God (2 Timothy 3:16), to Jesus Christ (John 1:1, 14), to an angel (possibly Gabriel, who was the announcing angel of Hebrews 1:7 and the messenger of God), and to the apostle John (Acts 1:13). This is the progression of the Word to humanity revealed and illuminated by the Holy Spirit (2 Peter 1:19–21).

The urgency of the message for the **terminal generation was** captured in the initial words of the Scripture, those things that must shortly come to pass,(Rev.1:1) and it has now been 2,000 years since these prophetic words were given. A great illustration of this is found in Jesus' parable about the stewards in Matthew 25:14–19 from the Olivet Discourse; its context was **the last days and the pending return of Christ in glory.**

A parable is an earthly saying with a heavenly meaning, and Jesus Christ made extensive use of parables in His teaching and preaching for several reasons. First, His Jewish audience comprised the religious leaders of the day—the Pharisees, Sadducees, scribes, and Herodians who rejected Christ's message and wanted to arrest Jesus for His teachings, sermons, miracles, and actions (Matthew 22:45–46). At that time, Jesus began to teach with parables designed to reveal and conceal.

Second, the Bible records the various disciplines by which the nations were instructed: "For the Jews require a sign [miracles and healings], and the Greeks seek after wisdom [parables and allegorical lessons] to rouse the intellect" (1 Corinthians 1:18–25).

Likewise, in the apostle Peter's second epistle (2 Peter 3:1–9), we read about the skeptics concerning the return of Christ. God is not bound by time but by His promise; God's Word is truth. How many *generation Xers and millennials think of the imminent return of Christ? Christ's* return for His church will be sudden, soon, swift, and silently unseen by a lost and dying world of skeptics and unrepentant sinners.

This testimony of the parable of Christ in Matthew 25:14–19 and 2 Peter 3:1–9 renders the idea of "Surely I come quickly" (Revelation 22:21) in a clear and understandable light. (For further study on end-times parables, read Matthew 21:33–41, **the parable of the vineyard;** Matthew 25:1–13, **the parable of the ten virgins;** Luke 14:16–24, **the parable of the great supper;** and Luke 16:19–31, **the parable of the rich man and Lazarus.**)

In verse 2, we read of the truth of the record revealed in the testimony of Jesus Christ. One of the many names Jesus Christ used in Scripture to identify Himself was the "Word of Truth" (John 14:6). Every attribute of God the Father, Son, and Holy Spirit, the Trinity, is complete and full perfection. The essential character, nature, personality, thoughts, and actions of God, Jesus Christ, and the Holy Spirit are perfect, brilliant holiness. Of all the communicable and incommunicable attributes of God and the Trinity, holiness is first; all God's other attributes magnify and illuminate His holiness like a shining light on the center stage of time and eternity. Jesus Christ is the way, the truth, and the life (John 14:6), and the Word of God is perfect truth (John 1:1–3). Some things are impossible for God; He cannot lie or to break His promises or Word (Titus 1:1–2).

In verse 3, we read the special blessing that those who read it, those who hear it, and those who keep the words of this prophecy will receive. All Scripture is inspired of God (literally translated as "the God-breathed Word") to man, and the Word is profitable for doctrine, for reproof, for correction, and for instruction (2 Timothy 3:16–17), and it can make us wise unto salvation (2 Timothy 3:14–15). Yet, this book yields a special, God-given blessing for its study, meditation, and obedient observation.

Some additional verses about the Word of God are Psalm 119:11, the Word hidden in our hearts will keep us from sin; Psalm 119:105, the Word of God is a light and lamp to guide us in life; Hebrews 4:12, the Word of God is powerful; Revelation 19:15, the Word of God is a sword of defense to rebuke the adversary; Deuteronomy 8:3, the Word of God is the Bread of Life; Ephesians 5:26, the Word of God is a washing water; and Jeremiah 23:29, the Word of God is a consuming fire and a hammer.

Why is there a blessing in this book? The answer is in the Old and New Testaments in Haggai 1:2 and 2 Corinthians 6:2: "Behold today is the day of salvation." This certainly addresses the **terminal generation,** and it relates directly to the prophetic words of Revelation 1:3: "The time is at hand." The **parable of the rich fool in** Luke 12:16–21 is appropriate reading during this portion of our study. No obituary ever reads, " … and he died tomorrow." As the Bible declares, there is a day appointed unto all of us to die, and although you might have tied your shoes this morning, the undertaker may untie them tonight.

Verse 4 gives us the addressee of the letter, the seven churches. Each represents a specific New Testament church in the first century and represents an epic period in the history of the church age these past twenty-one centuries. We will study the seven churches in detail and the time frame represented according to the Word and history of prophetic fulfillment in chapters 2 and 3.

A familiar statement of truth is found in the Gospels and the epistle letter of the apostles, "Grace be unto you and peace, from him which is, which was, and which is to come." We receive grace and peace from God the Father by accepting His Son, Jesus Christ, as our personal Lord and Savior. Grace is the gift of God (John 3:16–17) at the expense of His only begotten Son (Colossians 2:13–14), who gave His life for sinners on Calvary's cross 2,000 years ago (Isaiah 53:1–5). Peace is the blessing of salvation through Jesus Christ alone (Ephesians 2:8–9) and our Prince of Peace (Isaiah 9:6–7), and it is the peace of God in place of the wrath of God upon human souls (Romans 5:1). The chastisement of our peace was upon Him when He took away our condemnation (Romans 8:1). The grace, mercy, and peace of God is bestowed upon repentant sinners by the power of the Holy Spirit that indwells and seals the human heart at the moment of salvation (Ephesians 1:10–14). This is often defined for us in Scripture as the b**aptism of the Holy Ghost.**

Bible doctrine does not teach a second work of grace or salvation, nor is the baptism of the Holy Ghost in the present church age demonstrated by speaking in tongues. The baptism of the Holy Spirit is solely and uniquely the work of God within the human heart. A person is baptized once by the Spirit of God, but the filling of the Holy Spirit should happen frequently and repeatedly in a maturing Christian life. Someone asked the late, great D. L. Moody, "Why must a person be filled with the Spirit more than once?" Moody answered, "Dear lady, we must be refilled often, we leak."

Revelation covers the past, present, and future state of Christ's churches.

There were seven spirits before His throne. We will see many references to the number 7 in Revelation: seven spirits, lamps, horns, eyes, angels, trumpets, thunders, heads, crowns, plagues, vials, and kings. The number 7 in the Bible is representative of God's perfection, the number God used to define His works in perfection, completion, and fullness.

Sadly, many today delve into the occult practices of astrology, kabbalah, Masonic lodges, channeling of spirits in the new age movement, horoscopes, hypnotists, and the study of numbers to discover a divine, hidden code in the Bible. The well-known actor Tom Hanks was the main character in the movie *The da Vinci Code*, which involved searching for hidden codes in the Bible. When people become involved in this nonsense, it leads only to the destruction of their faith. The Bible is clear, concise, and straightforward. God was succinct in His presentation of the infallible Word, and there is nothing hidden that shall not be revealed (1 Corinthians 14:33). We will discuss later Satan's number, the number of man, 6, and it will always fall one short of perfection; it pales in comparison to God.

This portion of Scripture speaks of the perfection of the third person of the Trinity's personality, person, and actions. The Holy Spirit is a Spirit of power, gifts, light, conviction, encouragement, strength, wisdom, love, and preservation.

Verses 5 through 8 in Revelation 1 give more titles for Jesus Christ than any other book in the Bible. These are the first twenty-four titles for Jesus given in Revelation. Revelation also contains more Old Testament quotations and allusions than any other New Testament Book, 377 in total from Genesis to Malachi. The term for this repetition is *recapitulation,* God repeating His message. God's messages remain without confusion or change from the beginning to the end of the book. You will find no contradictions or errors in the Word of God.

Among these titles are Jesus Christ (1:1), the Faithful Witness (1:5), the First Begotten of the Dead (1:5), the Prince of Kings of the earth (1:5), the Alpha and Omega (1:8), the First and the Last (1:17), and the Son of man (1:13).

Jesus loves us with an *agape* **love, perfect and full,** and therein is the message of the Bible and Revelation. God sheds His love in our lives when we receive Jesus Christ as our Savior, and He removes our fears and confusion. Jesus washed away our sins (Hebrews 9:22; Ephesians 5:26). He appointed us kings and priests unto His Father. Note that Jesus was identified as God or the I AM of Exodus 3:14 and the I AM of the seven allegorical statements of Jesus as recorded in the apostle John's gospel letter. We will serve the Savior in eternity, and heaven will not be boring. In this present day, in our daily lives, we must strive to do all things as unto the Lord, study to show ourselves approved of God (2 Timothy 2:15), and be prepared to give a witness of the hope in us and serve the cause of Christ (1 Peter 3:15; Romans 12:1–2).

Verse 7 is a prophetic quotation from Zechariah 12:10 and Acts 1:9–11: "He shall come in the clouds and they shall look upon him whom they pierced." Jesus Christ in His **passion,** during the course of the seven unjust and illegal trials before the high priest, before Pilate, before Herod, and before the crowd gathered in slander against Him, fulfilled the prophecy of Isaiah 53:1–12. The Lamb of God was pierced by the cruel hands of men, His beard was plucked from His face, His brow was pierced by the crown of thorns, His flesh was torn from His body by the Romans' scourges, His wrist and feet were pierced by Roman nails, and His side and heart were pierced by the centurion's spear. The details of Christ's suffering for our sins is more gruesome than our thoughts can imagine, although the prophets throughout the ages have described for us in vivid detail the torture Christ endured to set us free from the slave market of sin and degradation as repeatedly noted in Scripture.

- Isaiah 52:14: "His visage was so marred more than any man, and his form more than the sons of men." The brutality inflicted on Christ made him unidentifiable to the mob, and Pilate had to declare, "Behold the man," since Jesus' body had been reduced to a mass of bleeding, torn flesh. His face was so swollen from the beatings and the raging fever of dehydration and thorn poisoning that He could no longer be recognized as the Messiah, the King of the Jews, the carpenter's Son.
- Isaiah 53:5: "Because he hath poured out his soul unto death, and he was numbered with the transgressors, and he bare the sins of many, and made intercession for the transgressors."
- 1 John 2:2: "And he was the propitiation for our sins, and not for ours only, but also for the sins of the whole world."
- 2 Corinthians 5:21: "For he hath made him to be sin for us, who knew no sin: that we might be made the righteousness of God in him."

Verse 8 is one of the many passages in Revelation we will study that confirms Jesus Christ is eternal, self-existent, as is God the Father and the Holy Spirit. Many in today's world religions, including Islam, Mormonism, and Jehovah's Witnesses, will not deny the existence of Jesus Christ, but they fail to recognize His deity of eternality, the fact that He is the only begotten Son of God who was incarnated by the Holy Spirit moving upon the Virgin Mary. Sadly, to their destruction, they deny the visible and bodily resurrection of Jesus Christ.

In verse 8 Jesus Christ took the name of God, *El Shaddai,* **the Almighty God,** from Genesis 17:1. The apostle Paul recorded for us in his epistle to the Philippians,

> Let this mind be in you, which was also in Christ Jesus. Who being in the form of God, thought it not robbery to be equal with God. But made himself of no reputation, and took upon him the form of a servant and was made in the likeness of men. And being found in fashion as a man,

he humbled himself, and became obedient unto death,
even the death of the cross. (Philippians 2:5–8)

This passage reveals the **hypostatic union of God and man.** Jesus Christ was all God, sinless, and holy (2 Corinthians 5:21), but He was also human by His incarnation (John 1:14). Because of Christ's sinless life, by His keeping all the laws and commandments, and His obedience to the Father, Christ ransomed us from sin; He redeemed us. Jesus Christ was the only one eligible to redeem fallen humanity and to pay the ransom for sin. There are four reasons this was possible.

1. Jesus Christ was not under the calamity of sin since Jesus was sinless (2 Corinthians 5:21).
2. Jesus Christ was our near kinsman redeemer as required by the law. Galatians 4:4 states that Jesus was born in the fullness of time, born under the law, and Isaiah 7:14 tells us, "Therefore the LORD himself shall give you a sign, behold a virgin shall conceive, and bear a son, and shall call his name Immanuel." Immanuel translates as "**God with us.**"
3. Christ was the only one qualified to pay the full redemption price for sin for all humanity for past, present, and future sins (1 John 2:2; Hebrews 9).
4. Christ was the only acceptable sacrifice to God for original sin and all other sin. God brought His own sacrifice to the mercy seat of heaven for our sins, His Son, Jesus Christ, the Lamb of God (John 1:29).

Verses 9 through 20 explain the Patmos vision. John identified himself with fellow believers who would receive these letters as brothers in Christ, companions in tribulation. No doubt John remembered Jesus' words in John 16:33: "In this world you will have tribulation, but in me you might have peace, but take hope, I have overcome the world." Peace is a choice in life. Regardless of the afflictions, trials, tests, persecutions, or flaming arrows of the adversary, we can choose to have peace in Christ Jesus, knowing His grace is sufficient (2 Corinthians 12:9).

John did not lament exile on Patmos. He wrote, "I am here for the Word of God and the testimony of Christ." Have you ever been somewhere uncomfortable, cold, hot, tired, secluded, isolated, lonely, dark, or dangerous? You probably cried out to God, "Why me?" and God responded, "I have chosen you."

Our times of trials and tests are for our instruction, perfection, protection, or in some cases for punishment or prevention. Our trials often reflect the trust God places in us as His servants, and it is not necessarily the trust we have in God. Job is the oldest book in the Bible; it predates Genesis, as the Bible is not arranged chronologically. This does not diminish the accuracy or authority of the Word of God. It is most appropriate that this oldest book opens with the theme of the testing of the righteous, Job, by our adversary, Satan.

God allowed Job to be tested and tried by Satan, and although Job was not privy to the heavenly conversation between God and the devil, he remained faithful to God and never faltered in his righteousness before God even in the midst of his satanic trials and tribulations. Job said, "The Lord gives and the Lord takes away, blessed by the name of the LORD, and in all this, Job sinned not."

Later in our studies of the two witnesses in Revelation 11:3–12 that stand before God at the Western Wall in modern-day Jerusalem, we will see once again the level of trust God places in His servants.

John is in the spirit, not a ghost but fully consumed by God and Jesus Christ, and they are all that matter to him. John is oblivious to any distractions. One of the curses of the twenty-first century is the noise of social media, cell phones, texts, Twitter, Facebook, the Internet, and twenty-four-hour television. These can become all consuming and distract people from what is of paramount importance, a right relationship and fellowship with God and Jesus Christ. Such distractions can drive people away from the Word of God.

In Amos 8:11, we read, "Behold the days come saith the Lord God, that I will send a famine in the land, not a famine of bread, nor of a thirst for water, but of hearing the Words of the LORD." Sadly today, many Bibles have gone unread by the past two generations in America. Some Bibles have thousands of miles on them only because they never leave the car except to be carried for show on Sunday. We can wear out cell phones every six months, but our Bibles have been with us since childhood for lack of use. The late, great preacher and evangelist J. Vernon McGee stated in his "Talk through the Bible" radio program, "Possibly the greatest dust storm in America since 1935 would be if all the Christians would pick up their Bibles at the same time and dust them off." Sad but true. In today's **terminal generation,** we can google anything in under ten seconds but cannot locate the Book of Esther in the Old Testament. Ah, "for such a time as this."

Christ commanded John to write all that he saw and send it to the seven churches Jesus had selected: Ephesus, Smyrna, Pergamos, Thyatira, Sardis, Philadelphia, and Laodicea. Voices like a trumpet came from behind John in verse 10, and John turned to hear and see. We must always turn and face Christ humbly because God rarely shouts at His children, and we reverence God by listening to His still, soft voice with rapt attention.

Note that in the vision of the seven candlesticks and the seven stars, the stars are in the right hand of Jesus.

John described Christ as clothed in a robe to His feet, a golden girdle—a wide belt or sash—around His waist. His hair was like white wool, and His eyes were flames. His feet looked like fine brass. He had a booming voice like many waters. Note that Jesus had a body, and although it was glorified, it bore the marks of the thorns on His brow, the nails that pierced His hands and feet, and the spear that pierced Him.

John saw Jesus Christ not for the first time. John had walked with Jesus for three and a half years during His ministry on earth. John witnessed the transfiguration of Christ on the mountaintop with Peter and James. John was present at the crucifixion and was witness to Jesus' resurrection and ascension. To be in the presence of Jesus was overwhelming; the text tells us that John fell down as if he were dead. Christ's most frequent command in the Scriptures was, "Fear not." We do not need to fear Jesus Christ, but we must receive Him as our personal Lord and Savior, and like His disciples, we must follow Him faithfully.

Jesus commanded John, "Fear not, for I am alive evermore and have the keys of hell and death." I'm sure John did not realize at the time the prophetic nature of the words *hell and death*.

There are five keys mentioned in the New Testament, and our Lord carries all of them. They are the **keys to the kingdoms** (Matthew 16:19), the **key of knowledge** (Luke 11:52), the **key of the throne of David** (Revelation 3:7), **the key to the bottomless pit** (Revelation 9:1, 20:1), and as mentioned, the **keys of hell and death.**

John received the command to write the a**pocalyptic and prophetic words of Jesus Christ about the end of the age. Jesus explained t**he mystery of the seven candlesticks and the seven stars as the seven pastors of the seven churches.

Part II

The Letters to the Seven Churches: Revelation Chapters 2 and 3

In Matthew's gospel, Jesus Christ asked His disciples who people said He was. The disciples responded with various answers; some said He was John the Baptist, some said Elijah, and others Jeremiah or one of the prophets. Jesus asked, "Whom say ye that I am?" Simon Peter said, "Thou art the Christ, the Son of the Living God." Jesus said,

> Blessed art thou Simon Bar-jona: for flesh and blood hath not revealed this unto thee, but my Father which is in heaven. And I say unto thee, that thou art Peter, and upon this rock I will build my church, and the gates of hell shall not prevail against it.

Jesus' church was bought, built, and paid for by His shed blood and suffering on the cross. In Matthew's gospel, we find several points of interest before entering our study of the seven churches of Revelation 2–3.

The creation of the church, the called-out assembly of born-again, baptized followers of Jesus was a future event that would follow His passion, death, resurrection, and ascension. During His forty days of ministry following His resurrection, Jesus revealed Himself to the apostles, the disciples, and the general population in fulfillment of His words of prophecy in John 2:19: "Jesus answered and said unto them, destroy this temple and in three days I will raise it up."

In Luke 24:46–49, Jesus gave the apostles and disciples the Great Commission of the church and told them to wait in Jerusalem for the promise of the Father until they received power from on high. This passage restated Christ's message to the apostles in the upper room concerning His impending death, burial, and resurrection and the promise to send the **Holy Ghost.** Ten days following Christ's ascension, on the day of the Feast of Pentecost, God sent the Holy Spirit to indwell, seal, and secure the hearts and souls of all born-again believers in the gospel of Christ. The Holy Spirit empowered and equipped the saints for the ministry of the church Jesus Christ established.

The church was to be built upon a rock, Jesus Christ, the only sure, safe, and secure foundation for a church to stand and endure. It is necessary to look to the original language to understand this passage. The original manuscripts offer a play on words: "Thou art Peter [*petros, a little rock*], and upon this Rock [*Petra*] I will build my church." Christ is careful to tell us the church is not founded on the apostles but on Jesus Christ, the *Rock of Ages.*

In many scriptural passages, Christ is the Rock. In 1 Corinthians 10:1–4, we read that Christ was the spiritual Rock that followed Israel in its wilderness journey. In 1 Peter 2:1–8, we learn that individual believers are lively stones, and each one is part of the spiritual house that makes up the body of the church, but Jesus Christ is the cornerstone, the head of the church (Ephesians 5:23).

Revelation 2 opens with a very personal address from Jesus Christ to the seven first-century New Testament churches that symbolically represent the church at a specific time in the full expanse of the church age from AD 33 to our present churches in this **terminal generation.** Have you ever wondered why Jesus wrote to the Christian churches and not to Israel in Revelation 2 and 3? Remember Luke 13:30, "The first shall be last and the last shall be first"? If we keep this thought in mind, it will help us grasp the Great Commission Jesus Christ entrusted to born-again believers to spread the gospel to the world.

God called Israel a chosen people unto Himself (Genesis 12:1–3) to tell all the nations of the world about God, His Word, and His promises to send a Redeemer to bless all nations. But in time, Israel became as pagan as its neighbors. The priests who were to serve as earthly examples of godly behavior became as corrupt, evil, and perverted as pagan priests. The sins of the nation included transgressions and iniquities before God; the sin of idolatry; the sins of adultery and immorality; the sin of the oppression of the poor, helpless, and strangers in the land; and the sin of corruption for personal gain and favor with the people and surrounding nations. For their sins, God sentenced Israel and Judah to captivity by the Assyrian and Babylonian nations for seventy years.

When Israel came out of captivity, its people knew the judgments of God, but unfortunately, they moved from the ultra left to the ultra right and became nationalists and separatists who would no longer associate with Gentiles, sinners, the unclean, the poor, and the needy. They refused to assist widows and orphans; they chose to live by ceremony and legalism. Israel was no longer an effective tool in the hand of God to win souls so people would see His glory and receive His grace and mercy through Jesus Christ, their rejected Messiah.

This raises an interesting thought: have we limited God by our actions? Psalms 78:41 tells us that God indeed can be limited, souls can be lost, and nations can be destroyed because of humanity's **free will** and lack of obedience to God's Commandments and Christ's Great Commission. King Solomon wrote, "There is nothing new under the sun." These words of warning ring out loud and true today in our *pseudo-Christian churches* that appear to be godly but that deny God's power. Psalms 78:41 tells us, "Yea, they turned back and tempted God, and limited the Holy One of Israel."

How do we limit God? We do so when we fail to tell the next generation about God from the Word of God (Psalm 78:1–7; Ephesians 6:4). We have lost our last two generations in America by not preaching God's Word and by removing prayer from public schools, courthouses, state houses, the White House, and sadly from our own homes and families. We have removed the Bible from classrooms, and the Great Gideon organization must now pass out the New Testament on sidewalks away from school property. Our nation fears lawsuits more than it fears God. We have taken the cross from courthouse lawns and embraced a separation of church and state that our Constitution never implied or intended. Our founding fathers understood the oppression of faith and the necessity of the separation of the state from restricting private and public worship as a measure of safety so our nation could worship in freedom and truth without fear of reprisal, censorship, or incarceration.

We also limit God when we disobey His Word and yield to the pressure of being politically or socially correct at the expense of being in rebellion against God. God will not bless a mess (1 Samuel 15:23; Psalm 78:8–11). We limit God when we become unthankful and embrace a humanist view, an evolutionist view, or a worldview and no longer recognize the Creator and Sustainer of all life (Psalm 78:12–22; Romans 1:18–22). We further limit God when we backslide from His Commandments, statutes, ordinances, and words (Psalm 78:41).

God called out the church established by Jesus Christ and commissioned it and Christians with the ministry of reconciliation (2 Corinthians 5:17–20). The purpose was to fulfill the will of God (2 Peter 3:9) that none should perish but all should come to repentance. The church was to go to the poor and the wealthy, to the children and the adults, to the lost and the saved, to the blind, the maimed, the halt, the unclean and the healthy, to the criminal and the free, and into every segment of society, culture, race, and nation (Luke 14:16–24). It was to openly witness the gospel of Jesus Christ (Matthew 28:18–20; Acts 1:8) while living a Christlike life, separated from sin, sanctified, and loving the lost because Christ loves all (Romans 8:28–30; John 13:34–35).

As we study Revelation, we will see that indeed the last shall be first and the first shall be last (Revelation 4:1 with the soon-coming rapture of the church). This introduction to the seven churches and seven letters may seem strange at this time to you, but we must know and understand the value Christ placed on His church, which was His bride, and His ministry.

Jesus repeated a statement seven times in the letters to the churches: "I know thy works." These are sobering words as we realize we will all give accounts before God of our stewardship as Christians as well as a final account in this **terminal generation if we reject Jesus Christ as our Savior.**

Several Significant Points from Revelation 2 and 3

Each of the letters was addressed to the pastor (angel or star) of the churches (candlesticks from Revelation 1:20). Each letter followed a similar outline, but the contents were individualized. They included the specific church by name, the counselor identified as Christ, the commendation for the church, the condemnation of the church, the counsel to the church, the challenge to the church, and the church's age in secular history.

The First Letter—To the First Church at Ephesus: Revelation 2:1–7

The Church
Ephesus, the chief city of Asia, was the commercial and religious center of the region; it had a population of about 225,000.

The Counselor
Jesus Christ was identified distinctly in each letter to the churches. I am the one who holds the pastors [angels or stars] in my right hand and walk in the midst of the seven churches (Rev. 2:1)

The Commendation
Christ commended the churches on their works, labors, and patience and how they rejected false teachers and false apostles. Christ told them that they had persevered in the faith and that they should not give up or faint.

The Condemnation
Christ also told them that they were not perfect, that they had left their first love, Jesus Christ, the head of the church. God did not tell Adam to build the largest Sunday school, to evangelize the lost, or to become a missionary though these are worthy pursuits. The first thing God commanded was a right relationship, then sanctification, and then service. The church and Christians were to develop and maintain a right relationship with God the Father through Jesus Christ (John 14:6).

This holds true in our personal intimacy with God and in our marriages and families. I have counseled many couples whose marriages were in distress or already disastrous. Often, following a moment of opening prayer, I hand the couple a sheet of paper with a cross drawn in the center from top to bottom. I ask them individually to place a mark on the paper to represent how close they are to Jesus Christ's cross. Most often, the husband's and wife's marks will be on the opposite sides of the paper and far from each other's and the cross. We cannot be close to one another if we are not close to Christ. Those couples I saw put their marks at the foot of the cross didn't end up in divorce court.

In this first letter to the churches, Ephesus had focused on the church building, ceremony, traditions, and their labors, not on the cornerstone, Jesus Christ. Our God is a jealous God who will not play second chair in our lives, marriages, families, or nations.

One very familiar passage of Scripture, quoted in most wedding ceremonies, is 1 Corinthians 13:13: "And now abideth faith, hope, charity, these three, but the greatest of these is charity." The word *charity* translates as "love" and is the theme of 1 Corinthians 13, being repeated in verses 2, 3, 4, 8, and 13. This love is the *agape love, God's love, that* the church at Ephesus had forgotten. To capture the necessity of agape love, look at the conversation between Jesus Christ and the apostle Peter following Peter's denial of Christ. After His resurrection, Jesus set out to find His disciples and met them on the seashore (John 21:15–17). Jesus asked Simon Peter, "Simon son of Jonas, lovest thou me more than these?" Notice Christ choice of words; *lovest* in Greek is *agapas,* deeply loved, and meant to define a divine love (John 14:21) and the love that the royal law (James 2:8) demands (Luke 10:27).

Simon Peter responded, "Yea, Lord thou knowest that I love thee." Peter answered with the word *love* rendered in Greek as *phileo,* or "I am found of thee." It was a lesser degree of love than *agapas.* The conversation between Jesus and Peter went on for three full inquiries, but Peter still didn't get it. Why? Apart from the Holy Spirit of God indwelling a life and a heart, people cannot love as God commanded. The apostle Paul wrote in Romans 5:5, "Hope maketh not ashamed; because the love [*agapas*] of God is shed abroad in our hearts by the Holy Spirit which is given unto us."

Those without Christ will do only evil that will increase in proportion to their lust, greed, and desires. This does not mean they cannot exhibit brotherly love, *phileo,* or a sense of goodness and benevolence toward others, but they will not be able to exhibit God's love by keeping the commandment of Christ to love everyone as Christ lived and died for His church. This offers a great insight into the struggles within families, marriages, and homes today. Without Christ in the heart and home, people will follow their instincts that ultimately lead to divorce, abuse, addiction, desertion, violence, same-sex marriage, and abortion. The prophet Jeremiah wrote, "The heart is deceitful about all things and desperately wicked; who can know it?"(Jeremiah 17:9)

The importance of Christ's words to the church at Ephesus to return to its first love cannot be overstated. Throughout Scripture, we see the value God places on *agape love*. God's love was extended to us, and it is our salvation in Jesus Christ (John 3:16–17, "God so loved the world, that he sent Jesus"). God's love sent the **Comforter, the Holy Spirit, to** bring gifts to all men. In Galatians 5:22–23, the fruit of the Spirit is *agape* love, joy, peace, longsuffering, gentleness, goodness, faith, meekness, and temperance. Against such there is no law. It all begins with the gift of love, and out of love flows all the other gifts into lives, families, communities, and nations.

The Counsel
Christ wanted the church to remember three things: 1. Remember your heads and minds are to be given over to Christ. 2. Repent and give your hearts over to Christ. 3. Repent and give your hands and labors to Christ, or else I will come quickly and remove your candlestick. Notice today how many pulpits in America are empty because the Lord has removed His candlestick. In Ephesus today, there are no Christian churches within miles of the city; the area is smothered by Muslims.

The Challenge
The challenge is to him that has an ear to hear what the Spirit says to the churches. The reward is the Tree of Life, once in the garden of Eden but lost by Adam due to original sin and banishment but now available in heaven (Revelation 22:2).

The Church Age

The first-century church age ran from AD 33 to AD 95–100, the end of the apostolic era with the death of John the Beloved. This church in the sixty to seventy years following Christ's resurrection saw the evangelization of much of the known world through the power of the Holy Spirit as the apostles and disciples traveled the world as missionaries, evangelist, pastors, and teachers of the gospel. This age of the church closed with the completion of the canon of Scripture, our sixty-six books of the Bible.

The Second Letter—To the Church of Smyrna: Revelation 2:8–11

The Church

Smyrna was about forty miles from Ephesus and on a major trade route; it was home to many apostate Jews. Smyrna was celebrated for its many fine schools of medicine and science.

The Counselor

Jesus Christ identified himself as the First and the Last (eternality of Christ) who was dead (the cross and the tomb) but was alive (the resurrection).

The Commendation

Christ told the church at Smyrna that it had suffered poverty but Christ saw them as rich. Because Smyrna was an industrial city with many trade unions, these Christians were blacklisted from working because of their faith in Christ. Jesus warned (instructed) them that the persecution for their faith would last ten days. Ten days were a symbol for ten extensive periods of persecution by the Roman Empire.[1]

1. Nero (AD 64–68) was responsible for the death of Peter and Paul and many of the early church fathers.
2. Domitian AD (81–96) was responsible for the deaths of 100,000 Christians; he banished John to Patmos.

---

1   For additional study on the persecutions of the early church, see John Foxe (151 or Church Age 7–1587), *Foxe's Book of Martyrs*. The book is in its sixth printing under the ISBN 978-1-56563-781-8.

3. Trajan (AD 98–117) was the first to pass laws against the Christians; he burned Ignatius at the stake.
4. Pius (AD 137–161) was responsible for the death of Polycarp, an early church bishop.
5. Marcus Aurelius (AD 161–180) had Christians beheaded for his entertainment and had Justin Martyr executed.
6. Severus (AD 193–211) killed Origen's father.
7. Thracian (AD 235–238) was a brutal barbarian and commanded that all Christian leaders, pastors, and teachers be executed by the most brutal methods of torture and death.
8. Decius (AD 249–251) was determined to exterminate Christianity in the empire.
9. Valerian (AD 253–260) had Cyprian, the bishop of Carthage, executed.
10. Diocletian (AD 284–305) was the last and most severe persecutor of the church. For ten years under his reign, believers were hunted down, burned alive, fed to wild beasts, tortured, and put to death by every other cruel means imagined by men.

This hatred was vented upon Jew and Gentile Christians alike. When Titus besieged Jerusalem in AD 70 and leveled the temple and the city, he ordered all the Jews and Christians to be executed. It is estimated that 1 million perished in this slaughter. Secular history records Titus as lamenting there were not enough trees or land to erect crosses for the crucified bodies of the Jews and Christians. Most often, one body was nailed upon another (Romans 7:24: "Oh wretched man that I am! Who shall deliver me from this body of death?").

The Condemnation
Jesus Christ offered no condemnation to this church because its people had suffered and would suffer faithfully for the cause of Christ.

The Counsel
The counsel by Jesus Christ to the church at Smyrna was to be fearless and faithful and He would give them a crown of life, one of the five crowns mentioned in the Bible, and the promise they would not be hurt by the

second death. This was because the faithful followers of Jesus Christ had been freed from the wrath of God, had peace with God, and were free from condemnation (Romans 5:1, 8:1).

The Church Age

Though this letter went to the first-century church, it is symbolic of the experience of the Christian church from AD 100 to 313, when the persecution of the church by the Roman emperors ended. Through the **Edict of Toleration, sometimes referred to as the Edict of Constantine, The emperor** Constantine granted freedom to all Christians. The Roman Catholic Church was established at this time.

The Letters to Pergamos and Thyatira: Revelation 2:12–17

The Churches

These letters were once again addressed to the pastors of the two churches; the letters followed a similar outline but contained contents individual to each church: the church, the counselor, the commendation, the condemnation, the counsel, the challenge to the church, and the church period covered by the historic era. (A complete list of the church ages beginning with the letter to Ephesus and concluding with the letter to Laodicea appears at the end of this section.)

Pergamos was the political capital of Asia and was seventy-five miles from Ephesus. It contained one of the finest libraries of antiquity with over 200,000 volumes. Parchment was first used in Pergamos. Mark Anthony gave this library to Cleopatra.

The words of Paul the apostle to Timothy in 2 Timothy 3:7 are noteworthy for the study of this letter: "ever learning and never able to come to the knowledge of truth." Smyrna and Pergamos had great institutions of higher education and yet did not know the truth of Christ or the Word of God. Many of our current universities, colleges, and seminaries provide knowledge without wisdom, philosophy without theology, and science without Creation. Possibly the most dangerous ground for our eighteen-year-olds to stand on following high school is on the campus of secular and liberal universities or colleges. If children leave home without being instructed, grounded, and rooted in the Word of God, they are in Satan's sandlot of apostasy if they attend such educational institutions.

Proverbs 22:6 instructs parents, "Train up a child in the way they should go; and when he is old, he will not depart from it." As parents, we must raise and train our children from early on, when their hearts are tender, based on the Word of God. Ephesians 6:4 instructs fathers in their responsibilities: "Ye fathers, provoke not your children to wrath [don't discourage them], but bring them up in the nurture and admonition of the Lord." This passage instructs us to not discourage our children; rather, we are to give them an appetite for the Word of God and impart godly reverence and fear of the Lord to them. It is a fearful thing to fall into the hands of the Living God.

The Counselor
Jesus identified Himself to the church at Pergamos as the one who had the sharp sword with two edges (John 1:1, "the Word of God"; Hebrews 4:12, "the sharp and powerful sword of the Word of God"; John 14:6, "the truth of God's Word"; and John 1:14, "The Word was made flesh and dwelt among us and we beheld His glory, full of grace and truth"). The Word of God is the source of absolute truth and authority, and it is worthy of all study, meditation, acceptance, and practice.

The Commendation
Christ told the church at Pergamos that it had kept the faith even though its members lived in the city were Satan had his seat. For centuries, the devil carried out his empire in the world from Babylon (Genesis 11:1, Daniel 5), but when the nation of Babylon fell, Satan moved his throne to Pergamos. Among other idols, the city worshipped a giant snake (Genesis 3:1; Revelation 12:9–14, 20:2).

Satan's seat today is in the Middle East again (Daniel 9:27; Matthew 24:15) and will be in Babylon, from where he will direct the anti-Christ and the false prophet to erect his statue in the rebuilt tribulation temple in Jerusalem

(Revelation 13, 17–18; Daniel 9:20–27). This will take place during the tribulation period of three and a half years and the final three and a half years of the great tribulation. In the letter, Jesus Christ remembered and called out the name of one martyred for his faith, Antipas. His name does not appear anywhere else in Scripture, but this one commendation alone reminds us that Jesus Christ knows His sheep by name and deed. Christ also knows our names, trials, and afflictions.

The Condemnation

The members of the church at Pergamos were practicing the doctrine of Balaam, a doctrine of covetousness; their error was thinking they could control God's judgments and doctrine. (For additional study on a great Old Testament story of angels, curses, and the power of God, read Numbers 22. Even a donkey can see angels, and sometimes, God's simplest creatures are wiser than people. It's a great story.)

They were also practicing the doctrine of the Nicolatians, which God hated (Revelation 2:15), and by then, it was established in the church at Pergamos as doctrine. Many churches today practice the doctrine of the Nicolatians; it is defined as the **liberty to sin.** This ungodly doctrine in the church today is no longer referred to as the doctrine of the Nicolatians, but it is nothing more than the same old sin with a fresh coat of paint. We now call drunkenness the sickness of alcoholism, we call the misuse of drugs an addiction, and we call homosexuality an alternate lifestyle.

Our society is desensitized to sin and has grown gradually tolerant of that which is abhorrent to God. Sadly, Christian marriages today end in divorce as frequently as marriages among non-Christians do. *Generation X and millennial Christians* cohabit rather than marry, and the carnality of Christians in America today encourages them to gamble, drink, use illegal drugs, be worldly in dress and vocabulary, be greedy, gossip, slander, criticize, and deceive others. They indulge in pornography, adultery, and immorality and excuse it under the disguise of Christian liberty and eternal security.

Most likely, these Christians are *carnal at best, and most likely lost having never made Christ Lord of their lives* (Revelation 21:7–8). *Backslidden* is an interesting but often-misunderstood word; what many call a backslidden Christian is really a person who never slid forward to Christ and is still in a lost, sorry state, facing eternal torment. We have liberty in Jesus Christ, but never a license to sin!

The Counsel

Jesus wanted those in the church at Pergamos to repent or else He would come quickly and fight them with the sword of His mouth (Hebrews 10:31: "It is a fearful thing to fall into the hands of an angry God").

The Challenge

"To him that overcometh will I give" refers to hidden manna; this speaks of the special fellowship with Christ (the Bread of Life) from John 6:35 and 1 Corinthians 10:13. "A white stone with a new name" refers to the custom of the day employed by the judges to determine a verdict by placing a white stone and a black stone in an urn. If the white stone was drawn out, the person was found innocent. Paul wrote in Romans 8:1, "There is no condemnation on a person who is in Christ Jesus." We have been freed from the penalty of sin and the wrath of God because of our faith in Jesus Christ's death, burial, and resurrection (Romans 5:1).

The Church Age

Pergamos was a first-century New Testament church, and Jesus' letter symbolically reflected the church age period of AD 315–590.

The Letter to the Church at Thyatira: Revelation 2:18–29

The Church

Thyatira was thirty-five miles from Pergamos; the town had been founded by Alexander the Great around 300 BC. It was an industrialized union city and headquarters for trade guilds such as tanners, potters, weavers, dyers, and robe makers. Lydia was the first convert to Christianity in

Europe by the apostle Paul (Acts 16:14). Thyatira today has a population of about 25,000.

The Counselor
Jesus identified himself to the church as the Son of God who had eyes of fire and feet of fine brass, harking back to Revelation 1, when Christ identified Himself to John.

The Commendation
Jesus commended the church at Thyatira for its works, love, service, faithfulness, and patience.

The Condemnation
Jesus rebuked the church for allowing a false teacher, a prophetess symbolically called Jezebel, not the Jezebel of 1 Kings, but certainly a vivid typology of the murderous wife of King Ahab. Christ's primary objection to the church at Thyatira was that this woman had been allowed to teach in the church and was teaching men (1 Timothy 2:12–14). She was also teaching idolatry and immorality and was unrepentant of her sin.

God is not a respecter of persons—the souls of men and women are equally precious to the Lord, but the offices of pastor and teacher are reserved for men. We see in pulpits today women sitting in the office of a pastor bishop in defiance of the Word of God. This does not imply a woman cannot serve Christ, but Scripture is clear—men alone can be pastors and teachers (see 1 Timothy 3:1–7, Titus 1:5–9, and Titus 2:1–6 for qualifications for a pastor or teacher).

As punishment for having a false prophetess, the members of the church at Thyatira would go through the great tribulation, and those in its pews would suffer the second death (Revelation 20:14) at the great white throne of God. The church would serve as an example to other churches of the wrath of God against idolatry and immorality.

If it is not preached from the pulpit that salvation is by grace alone, by faith alone, by Christ alone, souls will perish generation after generation. The

Word of God is clear on these points (Romans 10:9–17; Ephesians 2:8–9; Acts 4:12; John 1:12).

The Counsel

Christ counseled those in Thyatira to not follow the depths of Satan, which Paul covered in part in Galatians 5:16–21 and Ephesians 6:10–18 concerning the fruit of the flesh and the armor of God. They are doubt, fear, disobedience, sin, self-righteousness, self-will, rebellion, and the buffet line of the world religions that reject the virgin birth of Christ, the incarnation and eternality of Jesus, His sinlessness, His death, burial, and resurrection that led to our redemption, and the inspired Word of God.

It is important to note that religion will not save a soul; it could send a soul straight to hell with a false sense of security. It is only by the grace of God and faith in the gospel message of Jesus that the brand is plucked from hell's fire.

Grace separates all world religions from Christianity. The late, great author and apologist C. S. Lewis wrote of entering a British conference room filled with theologians involved in a heated discussion. He asked what the argument was about. One theologian stated that they had been in the room for over a week trying to determine what separated other religions from Christianity, considering all had holy books, ascribed to a god or gods, had a sense of Creation and the worldwide judgment of the great flood, and spoke of an afterlife. C. S. Lewis responded, "It is quite simple. It is grace."

The Challenge

Jesus promised those in the church at Thyatira who overcome that He would give power and authority to rule over the nations and would give them the Morning Star (Psalm 2:9, Revelation 22:16). Born-again believers in Christ are promised to rule and to reign with Jesus in eternity, and by faith, we have the Morning Star, Christ, as we read in Matthew 28:20.

The Church Age

The church period covered was both the first-century New Testament church in Thyatira, which symbolically represented the church age between AD 590 and 1517.

The Letters to Sardis (3:1–6), Philadelphia (3:7–13), and Laodicea (34–22): Revelation 3

Sardis was thirty miles south of Thyatira, and was the capital city of Lydia. The city was well known for its great wealth; gold and silver coins were first minted there. Sardis boasted of large textile mills that produced carpets. The city was thought to be impregnable, but Cyrus the Great of Persia captured the city by following a secret path up a cliff in 549 BC. The city fell to Rome three centuries later. Sardis was all but destroyed by an earthquake in AD 17. These three historical events were the basis of Jesus' words to the church at Sardis in Revelation 3:3, **"Remember!"**

The Counselor

Jesus identified himself to the church at Sardis in verse 1 as His holiness, His position, and His authority, and He stated, "I know thy works and thou hast a name that thou livest and art dead." Historically, Jesus was using the illustration of the Roman census roles. At birth, a child's name was placed on the Roman province census tax rolls, but at death, his or her name was blotted out.

A sea shell is an excellent example of something that was once alive but is now dead. The shell that contained the sea creature is still intact, but the creature inside is long gone; only a faint echo of life remains. If we compare the first-century church at Sardis with the twenty-first century church in America, we will see great similarities. The great truths of doctrine, faith, and theology that were recovered during the *Reformation* have been surrendered again by the compromising church and its imposing programs and rituals and the multiplication of organizations that substitute for the Word of God and real spiritual life.

The business of the church is to bring life to the dead; the church is not to be a museum for the saints but a hospital for the sin-sick, dying world. The business of the church since the *Great Commission is threefold: to* evangelize the lost with the gospel's good news of Jesus' death, burial, and resurrection (Acts 1:8); to edify the saints in perfection and sanctification and conform to the image of Jesus (Ephesians 4:11–16; Romans 8:28–29); and to praise and worship God (Matthew 22:36–40).

In Revelation 3:2–3, Christ instructed the church to be watchful (1 Peter 5:8) and to strengthen those things that remained and were ready to die. The church at Sardis was critically ill but not necessarily terminal. Christ told the church to "**remember**" that pride caused Sardis to fail in 549 and 546 BC and that the city had been all but destroyed by an earthquake in AD 17.

I warn you of a final danger. The message for the churches today that crosses the bridge of time in our **terminal generation** would be, "Don't rely on yourself, but look to Christ and receive the promise and blessings of life."

There are stages of life in every church that may be seen from formation to closure. The first is its birth, characterized by childlike energy and enthusiasm for growth. It relishes the Spirit and enjoys Christ and fellowship. The second is its adolescent stage; it grows, experiences growth pains, and searches for its place in the body of Christ much like any teenager does. Third, during its adult years, it is grounded in the Word of God and embraces the Great Commission. At that point, the church is an effective tool in the hand of God; it grows and advances the kingdom of God.

A church will stay in this mature stage as long as its pastor and leadership practice and preach sound Bible doctrine and theology. It will be a teaching church with a sound *catechism for new believers, and it will* place high expectations on its members in terms of their service, witnessing, tithes, offerings, attendance, and prayer. Such a church will be in the world but not of the world; its members will separate themselves from worldliness and will be examples of Christ in their communities and homes.

A church in its mature stage will also send missionaries to foreign fields; it will have an active outreach ministry of evangelism to its community and will actively prepare young men and women for full-time Christian service as pastors, teachers, and servants of the Lord.

There is a fourth stage of a church, and this depicts the church at Sardis. Dramatic change marks this stage. If a church fails to hold fast to the Word of God in doctrine, theology, and practice, it will enter a stage of decline. It will no longer look to Christ in faith but look inward, and often, this will be reflected in the church as a tendency to *maintain* rather than *grow* its ministry. The focus of the church will move to finances rather than faith. It will no longer grow; it will allow attrition to lead it to its final stage.

This final stage occurs while the lights are still on and the doors remain open, but the life of the church is long gone. Only the formality of tradition and ceremony remain. Babies no longer cry in the nursery. Children no longer laugh in the sanctuary. Such sounds are replaced by the lamentations of aging and declining members who remember only the golden days of revivals and folks being saved gone by.

This reality is a stark testimony to the critically ill nature of most churches in America that report less than one salvation decision per year. The Southern Baptist Convention, the Holiness Churches of America, and the Non-Denominational Movement of the seeking churches stand today as exceptions to this statistic. They are still proclaiming to the **terminal generation** that it must be born again, that hell and heaven are real, and that there is one to shun and one to gain through faith in Jesus Christ alone.

My wife, Linda, and I were vacationing in Panama City, Florida, less than 720 miles from our home in Indiana. We enjoy Florida's panhandle, especially St. Andrews State Park and the white beaches. On our last trip, we were in Old Panama city's downtown, enjoying the architecture and shops. When we drove back to our motel, Linda said, "How sad." She pointed to a bumper sticker that read, **"I Was Born Okay the First Time."** The driver had possibly been hurt in a church, raised in an atheist home, abused as a child, or was an intellectual who rejected the notion of being born again. D. L. Moody said that to be born once was to die twice and that to be born twice was to die once. I agree.

In verses 4 and 5, Christ commended the church at Sardis as having a faithful remnant He knew. The word *names* carries us back to verse 1. This letter is a contrast between life and death, and Christ issued four promises in this letter to Sardis.

> Promise 1: You shall walk with me.
>
> Promise 2: You shall be clothed in a white robe of righteousness (Revelation 19:14).
>
> Promise 3: I will not blot your name out of the Book of Life (Revelation 20:15).
>
> Promise 4: I will confess your name before my Father and the angels in heaven (Matthew 10:32–33).

There are 6,683 promises in the Bible, and God has never broken one of them.

The Book of Life is one of four books in the Bible in which God keeps His record.

1. The Book of the Generations (humanity's linage that makes all humanity from Adam forward a recorded part of the human race, sinners by birth and nature).
2. The Book of the Law (humanity's recorded sins, transgressions, and iniquities that condemn humanity as guilty before God).
3. The Book of Works (humanity's attempt to become self-righteous).
4. The Book of Life, or the Lamb's Book of Life (humanity's salvation record as having accepted Jesus Christ's sacrifice for its sins).

Each of these books will come up in our study of Revelation 20:12.

To the Church at Philadelphia: Revelation 3:7–13

The Church
Philadelphia was thirty miles southeast of Sardis and had a large Jewish population. Philadelphia had been destroyed by an earthquake in AD 17 but had been rebuilt by Tiberius Caesar.

The Condemnation
The letter to the church at Philadelphia contained no condemnation but a precious promise. I have set an open door before you that no man shuts.

The Commendation
Christ commended the church for two of the most blessed things that can be said about a church: it openly confessed the inspiration of the Word of God as of divine origin (2 Timothy 3:16), and it openly confessed the incarnation of the Son of God (Isaiah 7:14; Micah 5:2; Matthew 1:18–25; Luke 1:26–36; John 1:14).

Church Age
Symbolically in the church age, the church at Philadelphia represented the **Great Awakening** and worldwide missions, worldwide evangelism, and the great revivals. Basic Bible truths were recaptured, and the doctrines of the inspiration of Scripture, the incarnation of Christ, the imputation of Christ, and the invitation of Christ were once again proclaimed and taught.

The Promises of Christ to the Church of Philadelphia

1. Hold fast because I come quickly, not soon but suddenly.
2. I have set an open door before you that no man shuts.
3. I will subdue your enemies.
4. I will keep you from the hour of temptation. What a great promise and precious promise for the **born-again believers in Jesus Christ**—the hope and assurance from the Word of God of our departure in the **rapture of the church** prior to the seven years of worldwide terror and destruction in the **end time.**

5. I will make you a pillar in the temple of my God (new Jerusalem), and I will write upon you my new name (unknown to us at this time in this present age).

Several words in these passages bear additional study, including *door*. There are four doors mentioned specifically in the Bible: the **door of service** (Revelation 3:8), the **door of the human heart** (Revelation 3:20), the **door of the rapture** (Revelation 4:1), and the **door of the Second Advent of Jesus Christ** (Revelation 19:11).

Jesus promised to make those who overcame a pillar in the temple. Although heaven is the temple of God, we are speaking historically as an example to the believers of the honor of having a pillar with their names inscribed on them for victorious service to the king. However, the name is literal; Jewish high priests wore a golden plate across their foreheads with the name *Jehovah* inscribed on it. We also will be identified as belonging to God, and though the hidden name of Christ is unknown to us at this time, we will one day know the intimate, special name of our Savior (Revelation 19:12).

To the Church at Laodicea: Revelation 3:14–22

The Church

The letter to the church at Laodicea is a sad final commentary of the last church of the last **church age.** Laodicea was ninety miles from Ephesus; its name means "*judgment of the people.*" The city had been founded by Antiochus II and was known for its immense wealth and its banking centers, theaters, and a medical school that was famous for its eye salve. Historical depictions of the city from the pages of history read like modern chamber of commerce advertisements seeking tourist and investments. The city was also known for its rich garments of black, glossy wool. In His plea to this church, Christ used each of these as an example of the illness of the church there.

The Counselor

Jesus identified himself to the church at Laodicea as faithful and true, the beginning of the Creation. Note this does not translate or imply that Christ had been created but rather affirms that Jesus Christ was present with God the Father and Spirit as part of the Trinity.

The Condemnation

Jesus Christ had no words of commendation for the church at Laodicea; He had only words of condemnation for their sin. Christ issued a call to repent and a promise to save all who would repent.

Several years ago, the great evangelist Billy Graham stated his concern for the fact that in the twentieth-century church, upward of 80 percent of the congregations were lost, dying, and headed to hell. I thought at the time that the 80 percent figure was alarmingly high, but now, having served as an evangelist and pastor in many churches in the Midwest, I think that 80 percent was too low. It may indeed be much higher today in our **terminal generation.**

Some time ago, as I was conducting door-to-door evangelism with a pastor for a day, I spoke with a man whose house was in a nice subdivision; it was well kept, and it had lovely landscaping. I introduced myself to him and invited him to visit with us at Englewood Baptist Church. He was not interested. I asked if I could ask him some questions, and he said that would be okay. "Sir, do you know Jesus Christ as your Lord and Savior? Have you made peace with God and accepted His great gift of Christ into your life? Do you know beyond any doubt that if you died today, heaven would be your home?" I told him that God wanted to meet his needs that day.

He became angry. "Do I look like I need anything? I own this home and a Lincoln and a Cadillac in the garage." When he slammed the door in my face, he slammed the door on his eternal destiny. He was unfortunately another lost soul of this **terminal generation.**

The pastor, who was standing on the sidewalk, asked me what the man had said. I repented of my answer later, but I told the pastor that the man had said he was headed to hell and was looking forward to the trip, that he was self-righteous, self-sufficient, and self-condemned by materialism, possessions, and pride. These sins have sent more people to hell than all others (Proverbs 29:1).

Christ's Words to the Church of Laodicea

Christ knew that their works were neither hot nor cold, that they made God sick just like drinking lukewarm water from Laodicea's mineral springs. In the 1920s and '30s, folks used to come to bathe in the **Pluto water warm mineral springs in French Lick, Indiana.** The water smelled like rotten eggs due to its high sulfur and mineral content, and though the water was potable, it was lukewarm and nauseating to the taste. I visited French Lick with my family on several occasions and am always reminded of Christ's letter to Laodicea.

Christ told the church that it said it was rich in goods, in need of nothing, and didn't know it was wretched, miserable, poor, blind, and naked—the five woes. Note that Jesus used Laodicea's geographical location as an example of its destitution. This really captures the heart of modern, materialist American churches with their massive building programs; the latest electronic devices in the sanctuary; bookstores at the entrance; coffee and donut kiosk welcome centers; sports centers; and golf, euchre, and softball tournaments. But they never preach confession, repentance of sin, or the reality of hell for the lost.

The Counsel
Jesus counseled the members of the church to get their daily needs from Him (Matthew 6:33), to open their eyes, and to realize that He loved them. The church had gone to sleep at the helm of a sinking ship. The *Titanic* was overloaded and lacked sufficient lifeboats, but on its maiden voyage made a damning declaration that God Himself could not sink the ship. The crew and passengers played music, rearranged the deck chairs, and carried on as though it would be alright. In less than two hours after hitting an iceberg, the ship slipped beneath the frigid waters of the Atlantic.

The church today has hit the iceberg of apostasy and is slipping away, oblivious to the warnings of prophecy and the Word of God (2 Thessalonians 2:1–12). It no longer declares the gospel of Jesus Christ or the end-time judgments on rebellious and sinful humanity.

Jesus gave the great verse of promise to confessing and repentant sinners who would open their hearts' doors and invite Him in as their Lord and Savior (Revelation 3:20): "Behold, I stand at the door and knock, if you let me in [free will], then I will come with you and you will sit with me in Heaven."

In 1969, I traveled Europe and visited several art museums. At one museum, an art critic spoke about a famous painting of Christ standing outside a home and knocking on the door. He said that the painter had forgotten to paint a door handle on the door. His observation was correct, but his criticism was in error. The painting represented the human heart, which must open from the inside to receive Jesus Christ. God will never barge into a life uninvited, but He will always extend the offer to be your guest, friend, and Savior. The church today needs to hear the knocking of Christ outside the sanctuary doors; He wants to get back into the church.

Another interesting observation about the painting of Christ knocking on the door was a constant reminder to me as I preached in nursing homes, trailer parks, and jails; I learned to be mindful of those in the shadows listening to the message but who were reluctant to draw near the crowd. If you study the painting closely, you will see the ghost image of the painter standing to the right in the bushes, looking and listening to see if the door will be opened. Many will not walk out of the shadows until they hear the Word of God, see the love of God modeled by the preacher, and are drawn to the altar by the Spirit of God. Come out of the shadows today and be saved.

Historical Time Line of the Church Age

Jesus was born when Caesar Augustus reigned in Rome and Cyrenius was the governor of Syria. Herod the Great was the king of Jerusalem at the time of Christ's First Advent (Matthew 2:1; Luke 2:1–2). When Christ suffered and died, Pilate was the governor of Judea, Herod Antipas was the king of Jerusalem, and Caiaphas was the high priest and son-in-law of Annas (Matthew 26:57; Luke 23:1, 23:6–8).

When Christ ascended to heaven in AD 33, the reign of Herod Antipas, who had had John the Baptist beheaded, was coming to an end, and the reign of Herod Agrippa, who killed James, was beginning (Mark 6:14–29; Acts 12:1–2).

The **church age** began on the day of the Feast of Pentecost fifty days after the resurrection of Jesus Christ and ten days following Jesus' ascension. This moment in prophetic history fulfilled the prophecy and promise of Jesus Christ to send the **Comforter, the Holy Spirit,** from God the Father to the church (John 16:7). It fulfilled the command of Christ for the apostles and disciples to tarry in Jerusalem until the Comforter came (Luke 24:49).

The churches listed below were historic, first-century century churches as identified in Revelation 2–3. They also represent a historic era in the church age from the past to our present and final church age for the **terminal generation.**

1. Ephesus was a church from AD 33 to 100, an age brought to a close by the death of John the apostle and the completion of the canon of Scripture.
2. Smyrna was symbolic of the period AD 100–313; the period closed with the Edict of Toleration, or Edict of Constantine, which brought an end to the ten periods of intense persecution of the church by the Roman Empire and formed the general church, known today as the Roman Catholic Church.
3. Pergamos was symbolic of the period AD 315–590 and closed with the translation of the Bible by Jerome into Latin.
4. Thyatira is symbolic of the period AD 590–1517. This period covered the Dark Ages but closed with the rapid spread of the written Word of God. John Wycliffe translated the Bible into English, John Huss was a fearless preacher of this era who honored the preaching of the Bible, and William Tyndale printed the first

copy of the New Testament in English, providing commoners the Word of God.

5. Sardis is symbolic of the period 1517–1700, the time of Luther's Reformation.

6. Philadelphia is symbolic of the period 1700–1900; it is considered the Great Awakening of preaching, evangelism, and missions. Notable Christian leaders of this era were Jonathan Edwards, John Wesley, George Whitefield, William Carey, Adoniram Judson, David Livingston, Charles Spurgeon, and D. L. Moody.

7. Laodicea represents this present church age, from 1900 to the present. The characteristics of this age are captured in the seventh letter to the churches (Revelation 3:14–22). If there is one word to describe this era, it is *apostasy*!

PART III

THINGS THAT SHALL BE HEREAFTER: REVELATION CHAPTERS 4–5

1. A door is opened in heaven, the rapture door—4:1–3
2. The enthroned elders—4:4–5
3. The four living angelic creatures—4:6–8
4. The elders and living angelic creatures worship the Lord—4:9–11

Revelation 4 reveals God gently preparing John the apostle for what would come. In this chapter, a change of location took place; John was transported from earth to the throne room of heaven. This was not a spiritual transportation but a physical change of location to heaven; Christ commanded John to "Come up hither and I will show thee things which must be hereafter" (Revelation 4:1).

John began this new section with the words *after this (4:1)*; the Greek phrase is *meta tauta*, "after these things," which was the closing of the church age with the final letter to Laodicea. The context of the passage is the rapture of the church, which occurs between chapters 3 and 4. The church was referred to no less than nineteen times in the first three chapters of Revelation, and it drops out of sight until chapter 19, at the end of the seven years of tribulation. As that time, the only godly group Satan could afflict and torment was Israel and those who rejected him.

Scripture strongly supports a pretribulation, premillennial rapture. This will be discussed in detail at the conclusion of this section, but the initial reference Scriptures are 1 Corinthians 15:51–57, 1 Thessalonians 4:13–18, 2 Thessalonians 2:1–3, and Revelation 4:1. John saw a door open in heaven (Revelation 4:1), heard a trumpet (1 Thessalonians 4:16), and heard a voice that called him up (1 Thessalonians 4:16).

In verse 1, John was called up to heaven, and his transport was immediate, in the twinkling of an eye (1 Corinthians 15:52). The Bible tell us that to be absent from the body is to be present with the Lord, and this refutes the false doctrine of *soul sleep*. The apostle Paul recorded the speed of our transport to heaven at the rapture of the church in 1 Corinthians 15:51–52.

> Behold, I show you a mystery, we shall not all sleep [die],
> because the Rapture of the church is for both the living
> and the dead in Christ, but we shall all be changed in

a moment, in the twinkling of an eye [a 1/10- second blink], at the last trump, for the trumpet shall sound, and the dead shall be raised incorruptible, and we shall be changed.

In verse 2, John saw the glory of the Father on the throne in heaven. Revelation is a throne book; the word *throne* is used in Revelation forty-five times, as compared to only fifteen times in the other New Testament books. John began to describe God but gave us no form. (John 4:23 gives us the details as Jesus Christ spoke to a woman at the well in Samaria.) God is Spirit, and we worship Him in spirit and truth. John described the appearance of God as a jasper stone, which is a white stone, and a sardine stone, a fiery red stone. These colors related to God's glory (God is all light and all holy) and His grace (God is merciful). These stones also are the first and the last stones of the twelve tribes of Israel the high priest wore on his breastplate.

Theologically, Reuben was the first tribe of Israel, and his name translates as "behold a son," which captures the incarnation of Jesus Christ, the Son of God. The last tribe of Israel descended from the youngest son, Benjamin, whose name translates as "the Son of my right hand" and signifies the glorification and deity of the Son of God, Jesus Christ.

In verse 3, John saw a beautiful green rainbow around the throne; this signified the coming judgments. Just as God's promise in his covenant with Noah by the setting of the rainbow in the sky was a sign that judgment by a worldwide flood would never happen again, John saw the green rainbow of the coming judgment of God on the horizon.

It is important to note Revelation and Genesis share much in common but contrast with one another. Revelation has often been called the book of re-creation. In Genesis, we read of the first creation, the first Adam, the first sin, and the first judgment, while in Revelation, we read of the last creation, the last Adam, the last sin, and the last judgment. God's plan for the ages—from eternity past to eternity future—is captured and revealed in the Bible, the wonderful message of the redemption of fallen humanity through the person and sacrifice of the Lamb of God.

In verses 4 and 5, John saw twenty-four elders seated around the throne of God. This raises interesting questions: Who are they? What are the crowns they were wearing? They were Old and New Testament saints, and although they were not identified by name, there is biblical evidence that they were the prophets and the apostles (1 Chronicles 24:3–5, 18; Luke 1:5–9; Revelation 21:12–14).

These were men, not angels, and they were wearing crowns. Martyr crowns are *stephanos crowns,* not diadem crowns worn by monarchs. This indicates the elders and apostles were those who had been slain for the Word of God. Jesus, the apostles, and the early church fathers charged Israel with the slaying of the prophets, and *Foxe's Book of Martyrs* records the historic details of the execution of the apostles by the pagan nations and the Roman Empire.

John the Beloved was the only apostle who did not suffer martyrdom but died a natural death. Interesting support of John's witness of heaven and seeing the glorified Christ was given in Christ's promise to John at Christ's *transfiguration* (Matthew 16:28): "You will not see death until you have seen the Son of man, coming in his kingdom." Among the slain prophets were Jeremiah, who was starved to death in Egypt; Isaiah, who was sawn in two; John the Baptist, who was beheaded; Stephen, who was stoned; the apostle Paul, who was beheaded; and the apostle Peter, who was crucified upside down (Hebrews 11:37; Acts 7:51–52).

These seats are currently empty today in our generation, according to Daniel 7:9, and they will not be filled until the rapture of the church. Possibly, some seats remain to be filled by the greats of the church age, including Polycarp, Ignatius, Augustine, Clement, Martin Luther, C. H. Spurgeon, D. L. Moody, and Billy Graham. We don't know, but God does.

John saw and heard lightning, thunder, and voices coming from the throne of God. This spoke of the tribulation judgments to come. Why? If we look back to the initiation of John, we read, "I will show thee things which must be hereafter," after the end of the church age, after the rapture of the church. This is the terror for the **terminal generation** living today, shortly before the end. Why is this a terrifying and defining moment in time? The **rapture of the church is the trigger point for the tribulation and the revealing of the man of sin, the anti-Christ.** The apostle Paul gave a stern warning for those in the church today who have repeatedly rejected the Word of God, rejected the Son of God as their personal Savior, and quenched the Spirit of God that calls them to salvation.

In 2 Thessalonians 2:3, we learn that the anti-Christ, the son of perdition, will not be revealed until the rapture of the church. In verses 10 through 12 of this passage, the doom is presented to those of this generation who have rejected the call of God on their lives. Paul wrote,

> And with all deceivableness of unrighteousness in them that perish, because they received not the love of the truth, that they might be saved. And for this cause God shall send them strong delusions, that they should believe a lie, that they all might be damned who believe not the truth, but had pleasure in unrighteousness. (2 Thessalonians 2:3, 10–12)

We are speaking of a very select group of people living during this **terminal generation.** Paul addressed those who had heard the gospel as attending members of a church and yet had never committed their lives to Christ. This group will be left behind at the rapture of the church and never be saved. It is possible for men and women to sin away their day of grace (Proverbs 29:1; Romans 1:24, 26, 28, 32; Hebrews 12:16–17). We can only imagine the headlines the morning after the rapture of the church and the spin CNN will put on the missing millions worldwide: "Millions Missing In Alien Abductions," or "Flesh-Eating Virus Evaporates Millions Worldwide," or "Suspected Terrorist Nerve Gas Consumes Millions." But for sure, millions will be gone, the global economy will rapidly deteriorate, mass hysteria and anarchy will rule the streets of every nation, and the man of sin and his demonic plan to rule the world will be revealed.

Unfortunately, many who will have been left behind will celebrate and be glad all the Christians are gone.

At Mount Sinai, God gave Moses the Law with thunder, smoke, and His voice from heaven, and God prepares to judge sinful humanity for the laws they have forsaken and broken.

In verses 6 through 11, John saw a sea of glass similar to crystal. Glass is flat, smooth, and transparent, and we see the peace of heaven and remember the brass laver of Solomon's temple. Before entering the temple, priests had to perform a cleansing ceremony. We thank God that the laver of the Old Testament is turned to crystal in the New Testament, and we come before the Lord with peace, having been freed from sin and no longer in need of cleansing forgiveness.

This is speaking of our entrance into heaven. On Calvary, Jesus lifted His voice to heaven and said, "It is finished." Salvation's plan and the sin debt was paid in full, and atonement was made for all sin (1 John 2:1–2), past, present, and future.

Those who receive Jesus Christ as their personal Savior are *justified or freed from the penalty of sin* (Romans 3:23, 5:1, 6:23, 8:1). The Word tell us that as new believers grow in spiritual maturity, they are *sanctified or freed from the power of sin in their lives and are able to resist temptation to sin to a greater degree.* Once they die, they are *glorified and freed from sin.* Glorified saints have perfect peace with God that passes our understanding and can enter into the presence of God because of the finished work of Christ and the Holy Spirit in their lives.

John saw four living angelic creatures and noted the continuity of Scripture (Ezekiel 1:5–28 and Isaiah 6:2–3). These angelic creatures were intelligent, angelic, alert (eyes in front and back), and watchful. They were guarding the throne of God not in the sense that God was in danger but to continually proclaim what God is—holy, holy, holy! These creatures were angelic and represent the cherubim of Ezekiel 1 and the seraphim of Isaiah 6.

These angelic creatures' purpose in this passage was to reveal the eternal glory of the Son and the testimony of the four gospel records as seen in John's description of their faces. The face of the lion represented Jesus Christ as the King of Kings as recorded in Matthew's gospel account of Christ. The face of the calf represented Jesus Christ as the perfect servant branch in Mark. The face of the man represented perfect humanity, the *hypostatic union of God and humanity* as presented in Luke's account of Christ as the perfect person. The eagle represented the perfect deity of the Son of God as presented in John.

These living angelic creatures glorified and gave honor continually day and night without end, always alert and watching and praising God's eternality and His self-existence as the God of all creation. These creatures praised God for Creation and stated that God was worthy of glory, honor, and praise for all He created (Genesis 1:1–2:25; Psalm 19:1–6; John 1:1–3).

God created humanity in His image and gave humanity souls for the purpose of relationship with Him, the heavenly Father (Matthew 6:9–13). We were to fellowship with God, tend the earth, have dominion over the animals, multiply, and replenish the earth. The Lord was not compelled to create humans; He did so for His pleasure and to see humanity enjoy His creation as God intended it to be. God rejoices over us for He is good all the time.

The Rapture of the Church: Revelation 4:1

The disciples asked Jesus three questions in the Olivet Discourse (Matthew 24:25; Mark 13; Luke 21). Jesus answered two of the disciples' questions and revealed the signs of the end of times and elements of the coming great tribulation that carried them back to the writings of Daniel and other Old Testament prophets. To the disciples' question of "When shall these things be?" Christ said, "But of that day and hour knoweth no man, no not the angels in heaven, but my Father only" (Matthew 24:36).

Many have speculated about when Christ's Second Advent will occur, but only the Father knows. Christ has given us a road map of signs preceding the great and terrible day of the Lord spoken of in the Old and New Testaments. But concerning the rapture, the "catching away" of the church, we live in earnest expectation that it may be today, and we are instructed to listen for a sound and not look for a sign concerning the rapture. The sound is the shout of the Lord Himself, for the voice of the archangel, and for the blast of the trumpet of God (1 Thessalonians 4:13–18); the Lord Himself shall call us up by name, and we will meet Him in the air (Revelation 4:1; 1 Corinthians 15:51–57).

The Bible contains many typologies for our instruction and example in Scripture. In Genesis, we see the power and authority of God and a wonderful typology or word picture of the rapture in the life of Enoch. In Genesis 5:24, we read, "And Enoch walked with God and he was not, for God took him." This is a foreshadowing moment of the rapture of the New Testament church. Enoch walked with God, righteous and upright in his generation just as the church is to walk with Christ in its generation. At the appointed time, God caught Enoch away in the twinkling of an eye. This is essential in our understanding of the purpose of the rapture of the church. Enoch was taken by God in his generation before the judgment of God upon the whole world for sin in the worldwide flood. Likewise, in this present **terminal generation**, the church walks with and witnesses for Christ, and God will send His Son to rapture or catch away His followers before the seven years of the great tribulation.

The judgment of God is rapidly approaching; how much closer is the rescue and rejoicing of the rapture? The church that will be caught away to heaven comprises all **born-again, Holy Spirit–baptized believers** in the gospel of Christ since the day of Pentecost until the end of this present church age. At the moment of the rapture, there will not be one born-again believer left on earth—not one! There will not be one unborn child in the womb left on earth—not one! There will not be one child or adult who lacks the mental maturity to discern right from wrong left on earth—not one! The blood of the Lamb and the grace and mercy of God cover the infants and the mentally challenged. God will bring them with all the other saints.

Although the word *rapture* does not appear in the English translation of the Bible, the word *harpazo, the "catching away" or "gathering,"* is included in the original Bible manuscripts. The rapture of the church is the **next great cataclysmic event that will impact all humanity in this terminal generation.** The rapture of the church will affect every aspect of society, every nation, and every continent; the global economy will stutter and fail; the world will be in emotional and mental chaos; there will be worldwide panic, and anarchy will pervade the streets of every city as millions will be searching for family members. Civil unrest will result in martial law, and panic will ensue with the disappearance of untold millions known only to Jesus Christ and the Lord of the universal, blood-bought church.

How many Americans will attend church the first Sunday following the rapture? Who will be left behind to answer questions? Without a doubt, there will be preachers and priests left behind who never accepted Christ as their Savior. Deacons and elders will be left behind, as will be some piano players, organ players, and Sunday school teachers who will show up just as always. These people never trusted God's plan of salvation; instead, they trusted in their self-righteousness, church membership, baptism, church tradition and ceremony, and the golden rule as though they could merit heaven on their own.

Word choice is always a potential danger in preaching, teaching, and writing. The late J. Vernon McGee was fond of saying, "Keep the cookies on the lower shelf so the children can reach them." I know everyone who reads this book may not be a Christian or possibly never had the opportunity to attend church and much less a Bible college, so I will choose and define my words carefully and clarify those of a theology (Christian Lingo Nature).

What does it mean to be *saved*? This word is synonymous with elect, redeemed, justified, born again, or reconciled to God through Jesus Christ. The word *lost* describes those who have never confessed their sins, repented, or turned from their sins and asked Jesus Christ to be Lord of their lives and followed Him obediently, faithfully in a sanctified (maturing spiritually) and a God-fearing and honoring life. To be lost means to reject the gospel message of Jesus' death, burial, and resurrection in payment for our sins.

Concerning the rapture of the church, note that the church is referred to in Scripture as the called-out ones, the bride of Christ, the assembly, and most often simply the church. The church, or *ekklesia in Greek, comprises* all born-again living and dead in the universal church since the day of Pentecost and all the born-again believers fellowshipping today in Catholic and Protestant churches.

The church was established on the day of Pentecost, fifty days following the resurrection of Jesus Christ and ten days after His ascension to heaven in fulfillment of Bible prophecy. Matthew 16:18 records in the words of Christ that the birth of the church would be a future event following His passion, resurrection, and ascension. The birth of the church was a special gift from God; the Son of God promised to send the Holy Spirit to indwell all believers. This reflected a change from the Old to the New Testament. In the Old Testament, the indwelling of the Spirit of God was not corporate but individual; God selected prophets, priests, and kings to minister and lead.

At the arrival of the Holy Spirit in the upper room (Acts 2:1–12), we read of the promise of the Comforter; the Holy Spirit of God was revealed by the gifts of signs, miracles, and wonders in the early first-century church that confirmed the message and messengers of God to a lost and dying world. The giving of the Comforter was foretold in John 16:7–15 and explained by the apostle Paul in Ephesians 1:10–14.

The rapture of the church will be a uniquely Christian event; it will occur suddenly, soon, silently, secretly, and unseen by the lost world left behind. The rapture of the church will occur prior to the seven years of the great tribulation as promised by Jesus Christ in Revelation 3:10. The rapture will stand in stark contrast to Christ's Second Advent, which will be a bodily return of the Savior seen by everyone worldwide. His feet will touch down on the Mount of Olives in Jerusalem.

The rapture of the church will be an orderly event; our God is a God of order, and His Word is without error or confusion (1 Thessalonians 4:13–18). Paul instructed the young Christians in Thessalonica to not be troubled about their deceased family members because Christ had not yet returned. Paul gave these words of encouragement, comfort, and explanation. Their death will not prevent the rapture (Romans 8:38–39), and the dead in Christ (New Testament saints since Pentecost) will rise first from the graves, and then those of us who are alive and remain at the rapture will be caught up in the air to be together with the Lord forever.

It is important to understand the words of Solomon in Ecclesiastes 12:7: "Then shall the dust return to the earth as it was, and the spirit shall return to God who gave it." Solomon's words are a reminder to us (from Genesis 2:7) that God formed Adam out of dust and breathed life into him to make him a living soul.

Because of original sin of Adam and Eve, sin and death have plagued all humanity (Romans 3:23, 5:12, 6:23). In 2 Corinthians 5:8, Paul wrote that to be absent from the body is to be present with the Lord for those who are saved. Likewise, in Revelation 6:10–11, John wrote that to be in the Lord's presence prior to the rapture did not imply we were disembodied spirits. We will have a physical form until the rapture or resurrection, depending on the time of our death. New Testament saints are awaiting the glorified bodies they will receive at the rapture of the church.

It is also important to note that the rapture will be different from the first and the second resurrection of the dead in Revelation. The first resurrection will occur as stated in Revelation 20:4 and will involve the bodies of the tribulation saints who were killed for the cause of Christ. The Old Testament saints' bodies will be resurrected and united with their souls, replacing their intermediate bodies, and they will rule and reign with Christ for the thousand years of the millennium.

The second resurrection of the dead will not occur until the end of the thousand-year reign of Christ (Revelation 20:11–15), when the final judgment of the unrighteous dead at the great white throne of God will take place following the final rebellion by Satan against Christ. The unrighteous dead will be judged and doomed to eternal separation from God, without hope for pardon or parole, and they will spend eternity suffering the torments and terror of hell in the lake of fire for the sin of rejecting Jesus Christ as their Savior.

We must remember that in a very broad sense of the word, we all have *eternal* life. The great questions are not life or death but "Where will I spend eternity? What will be my final destination? Heaven or hell?" There is no door number 3. The choice is ours alone, and there is no doctrine of annihilation in the Bible; we will all spend a conscious eternity somewhere. John 3:36 states, "He that hath the Son hath life, and he that hath not the Son hath not life and the wrath of God abideth upon him already."

There are no elements of Bible prophecy or Scripture that must be fulfilled at this time that would prevent or prohibit the rapture of the church; that could happen before you lay this book down. The rapture is the next Bible prophecy to be fulfilled in this **terminal generation** in the fullness of God's time for the church age.

The Seven Sealed Book: Revelation 5

1. John sees the book—5:1–4
2. The character of Jesus Christ—5:5–7
3. The elders and the four living angelic creatures worship—5:8–10
4. The angels praise the Lamb—5:11–12
5. The universal adoration of the Lamb who is King—5:13–14

In Revelation 4, John was transported to heaven to the throne room and presence of God, the twenty-four elders, and the four angelic creatures. John saw seven things that filled him with awe and wonder. In Revelation 5, John witnessed an eighth event that caused his soul to be flooded with despair; the crisis of the **seven-sealed book began.**

In verse 1, "and I saw" was John's personal testimony as he was commanded to write in Revelation 1:19 of those things he has seen that were, are, and will be. John saw in the right hand of God the Father a book with seven seals. That book, according to many theologians, was actually a scroll that was the title deed to earth given to Adam (Genesis 2:8–17) but taken from him after he sinned (Genesis 3:22–24).

Many humanist philosophers and existentialists believe that if humanity lives in a perfect environment and receives perfect instruction, their lives will be perfect. The failure of this argument is not the creation of humanity, since God said it was good, but the desire of humanity. God made Adam lord over the garden with dominion over the animals. God created Adam in His image and gave perfect instructions to Adam that set the boundaries for life, peace, joy, contentment, and service. Adam had it all, but it wasn't enough. Adam and Eve wanted what had been forbidden, the fruit of the Tree of Knowledge of Good and Evil and to be like God.

The scroll had seven seals. Historically, the Roman Empire required all legal documents pertaining to life and death to be sealed seven times. When the chief priest and Pharisees came to Pilate following the crucifixion of Jesus, they reminded Pilate that Jesus had said, "After three days, I will rise again." The priest asked Pilate to make the grave secure. Sixteen guards surrounded the tomb, four on a side, and one on a side was always awake. A large stone was rolled across the entrance of the tomb, and a Roman seal was set upon the stone and the tomb as though it would prevent the resurrection of the Son of God. The penalty for breaking a Roman seal was death.

The stone on the tomb was not rolled away on resurrection morning to let the Savior out but to let us look inside and see the empty tomb, the grave clothes in a pile, and the napkin in a place by itself, assuring us that Christ had risen and was coming again (Matthew 27:62–66; John 20:1–10).

In verse 2, the angels proclaimed, "Who is worthy to open the book and to loose the seals thereof?" Although the angel was not named, this might have been Gabriel, God's announcing angel and messenger.

In verse 3, we read, "And no man in heaven, in the earth, under the earth was able to open the book, neither to look thereon." Let's follow the angel on his threefold search. He would have searched among the redeemed in heaven to determine if any were worthy to claim earth's title deed. Adam, Noah, Abraham, David, John the Baptist, Peter, and Paul were all ruled out because of sin. He would have search on the earth, but who on sinful earth could accomplish what no one in sinless heaven could achieve? Preachers, priest, kings and rulers were all unworthy because of sin. And certainly, if no angel could purify the earth, no sinner or demon of hell could either, for all have sinned and have come short of the glory of God. Therefore, the only one worthy to open the book was the sinless Son of God (2 Corinthians 5:21).

John's distress was recorded in verse 4; he wept because no one was found worthy to open, read, or even look into the book. John wept for three reasons, but what made it personal for him? He ultimately realized that his own resurrection, glorification, and earth's purification (with the removal of the curse placed upon the earth) was directly related to the contents and opening of the scroll. Sorrow, suffering, and tears have combined to carve out an ocean of human tears since Adam's tragic rebellion against God. Scripture and our own memories are reasons to shed tears.

In verse 5, we read, "But one of the elders [one of the twenty-four] saith to John, Weep not, For the Lion of the Tribe of Judah [Genesis 49; 2 Samuel 7; Luke 1] the root of David [Matthew 1:1; Isaiah 11:1, 10; Revelation 22:16] hath prevailed to open the book [scroll] and to loose the seven seals."

In verses 6 through 13, a praise and worship meeting broke out in heaven in honor of Jesus Christ, who was worthy. The Lamb of God (John 1:29) was seated by the throne of God; Jesus Christ is referred to twenty-nine times in the New Testament as the Lamb of God, and a special Greek word is used in this name, *arnion, a special lamb.* In the presence of God, the elders, the angelic creatures, and John, Jesus took the book from God. Those gathered around the throne served as witnesses to the transfer of this deed to its rightful owner, Jesus Christ.

Jesus was the Lamb of God slain for our sins, and He is characterized as having a metaphorical seven horns that speak of His perfection and power.

He was characterized as having seven eyes, referring to His knowledge of all things, and seven spirits, which speak of His sinlessness as the only begotten Son of God (John 3:16).

In verse 7, after Jesus received the book from His Father, a praise meeting began. In verse 8, the four beasts and the twenty-four elders prostrated themselves before the Lord. They played harps, and golden vials of odors (the prayers of the saints) were poured out before the throne. A saint's prayer flows before the throne of God and rises as a sweet, fragrant perfume. God saves our prayers and also our tears shed in this life; not a tear falls that God does not know about.

In verse 9, the four angelic creatures and the elders sang a new song, Thou art worthy to take the book and to open the seals thereof because, You were slain, you redeemed us to God by your blood out of every kindred, tongue, people and nations. This is the unlimited atonement of God for all repentant sinners.

In 1 John 2:2, we read that Jesus Christ was the payment for the sins of the world. This stands in conflict with the strict five points of **Calvinism** that state Christ died only for the justified. God is not a respecter of persons, and one sinner is no better or worse than another; all sin separates us from God equally, for we all have sinned and have fallen short of the glory of God (Isaiah 59:1–2; Romans 3:23).

Verse 10 contains the promise to the redeemed. We are redeemed to God by Jesus Christ to be kings and priests and to reign on earth. Notice the last words of this verse, *earth*. Earth will be our final destination following the new heaven and the new earth and the new Jerusalem of Revelation 21. Our intermediate destination is heaven, where God lives, rules, and reigns sovereign over the universe, but earth was made for humanity. We are terrestrial as well as spiritual beings, and we are designed and well fitted to serve in God's re-creation.

We will return with the Lord and rule and reign with Him in service and obedience on earth forever. The subject of heaven and all its particulars are presented in an excellent book, *Heaven*, by Randy Alcorn.[2]

In verse 11, the angelic choir began to sing; their harmonious voices certified in a number that cannot be counted by men, saying with a loud voice (and this reminds me of the psalm that reads, "Let the redeemed say so!") "Worthy is the Lamb that was slain to receive power, and riches, and wisdom, and strength, and honor, and glory, and blessings," the seven blessings of God to Christ.

In verses 12 through 14, John heard every creature in heaven, on earth, under earth, and in the sea saying, "Blessings to God who sits on the throne, and Blessings to the Lamb forever and ever." It is difficult to imagine such a choir and even more difficult to picture the animals singing, each in its own way praising God. Singing before the Lord has nothing to do with the quality of our voices but with the sincerity of our song to God. Music flows through the vocal cords but also from the heart and soul. And the four angelic creatures said, "Amen." At that time, the Spirit of God was so thick in the throne room that all the elders fell down and worshipped God.

---

2   Randy Alcorn, *Heaven* (Wheaton, IL: Tyndale House, 2004). This is one of the most concise, accurate and thought-provoking books about heaven available today.

PART IV

THE SEAL JUDGMENTS: REVELATION CHAPTER 6

1. The Lamb opened the first seal and the wrath of the Lamb was invoked—6:1
2. The first seal, a rider on a white horse, went forth to conquer—6:2
3. The second seal, a rider on a red horse, and peace taken from earth—6:3–4
4. The third seal, a rider on a black horse, and famine on the earth—6:5–6
5. The fourth seal, a rider on a pale horse, and death on the earth—6:7–8
6. The fifth seal, the martyred remnant—6:9–11
7. The sixth seal, anarchy on earth—6:12–17

In Revelation 6, the Lamb of God received from God the seven-sealed scroll, the title deed to earth. In chapter 6, the apostle John recorded the opening of the first six seals by Jesus Christ and the resulting judgments upon the earth and sinful humanity. Two significant periods are introduced in Revelation 6. The first period is the first three and a half years or 1,260 days of the **tribulation** in verses 1–11 and the beginning of the last three and a half years or 1,260 additional days of the last half of the **great tribulation in** verses 12–17. We understand these two periods from Daniel 7:13–28 and 9:20–27. Daniel's prophecy concerns his vision of the seventy weeks of years; it is of particular interest to the church today as the **terminal generation. We** are in the sixty-ninth week of years, and the rapture and the tribulation are quickly approaching. We can almost hear the hoofbeats of the *four horsemen of the apocalypse.*

In this portion of John's vision, the scene shifts from heaven back to earth as John sees the events of the seal judgments from heaven's portals. We must remember that not all the judgments of the seals, the trumpets, and the bowls were recorded in chronological order; some overlap these two periods. As we read the judgment chapters of Revelation, it almost defies our imagination and conscience to read of the terror and horrors that are about to be unleashed on God's creation. The high cost of sin is suffering, eternal death, and punishment for the unrepentant heart. God is holy, righteous, just, and loving, but He is also a God of wrath, and God's holiness demands punishment for sin.

Why are these judgments pronounced upon sin, transgressions, and iniquity? In Romans 6:23, we read, "For the wages of sin is death, but the gift of God is eternal life through Jesus Christ our Lord." Because of Adam's sin, all humanity inherited sin and death; all humanity became separated from God in relationship, fellowship, eternal purpose, and destiny. Romans 5:12 affirms this: "Wherefore, as by one man sin entered the world, and death by sin, and so death passed upon all men, for that all have sinned."

Romans 1:18–32 gives the vivid explanation and illustration of the sinful state of humanity in our **terminal generation.** In Romans 1:32, we read, "Who knowing the judgments of God, they which commit such things are worthy of death, not only do the same, but have pleasure in them that do them." This passage refers to the Gentile nations of the world.

Romans 2:17–3:8 gives the judgments on the sins of the Jewish nation for its members' sins. The Jewish nation of the twelve tribes and descendants of Jacob and Israel that sit in judgment over others are guilty of the same sin, self-righteousness before God.

Romans 3:9–23 refers to the whole world as guilty before God: "There is none righteous" (3:10), "For all have sinned and come short of the Glory of God" (3:23), and "They are without excuse" (Romans 1:20)

John 3:16–17 explains the grace and mercy of God and His plan for the ages, which had been prepared before the foundations of the earth were set to redeem fallen humanity. God gave everyone the opportunity to receive forgiveness of sin in the once-and-for-all atonement sacrifice of His only begotten Son.

> For God so loved the world that he gave his only begotten Son, that whosoever believeth in him should not perish, but have everlasting life. For God sent not his Son into the world to condemn the world, but that the world through him might be saved.

In verses 1 and 2, Jesus Christ opened the first seal, and John heard thunder (judgment was coming) much like spring thunderstorms that precede tornados. The sights and sounds were terrifying to John, but one of the angelic creatures encouraged John and instructed him to draw closer and see.

The counterfeit Christ, the anti-Christ, was riding a white horse; this was the anti-Christ mentioned in a hundred passages of Scripture. Daniel described the anti-Christ in Daniel 7:8–24, 9:27, and 11:21. John the apostle wrote of the anti-Christ in 1 John 2:18–22, 4:3, and 2 John 7. From the beginning of the early first-century church, Christians were convinced that a world ruler who was the embodiment of Satan would eventually come on the scene. Revelation 12–13 presents an **unholy trinity** that aligned Satan against the Father, the anti-Christ against the Son, and the false prophet against the Holy Spirit.

The real power behind the anti-Christ is Satan, the father of lies mentioned in John 8:44, and he is therefore the one who will condemn the multitudes to divine judgment (2 Thessalonians 2:11).

Revelation 6:2 instructs us that the one on the white horse went forth conquering and to conquer. This conquest will not be achieved militarily initially but rather by diplomacy as the anti-Christ assumes power and control of the European nations. His ability to conquer is apparent in his personal characteristics and skill as empowered and possessed by Satan.

1. He will be an intellectual genius—Daniel 7:20.
2. He will be an oratorical genius—Daniel 7:20.
3. He will be a political genius—Daniel 11:1, 4.
4. He will be a commercial/business genius—Daniel 8:25.
5. He will be a military genius—Daniel 8:24.
6. He will be an administrative genius—Revelation 13:1, 2.
7. He will be a religious genius—2 Thessalonians 2:4.

A great question asked and debated today in our present **terminal generation** is whether the anti-Christ is alive today. Certainly, the spirit of the anti-Christ is alive and well today; it is the Satan-inspired expression of lawlessness and rebellion against God, the things of God, and the people of God, Jews and Christians alike. It has been alive since Satan tempted Eve to doubt the Word of God. It has been the driving force behind the terrible history of the human race with its wars, murders, thefts, rapes, anarchy, and rebellion against the Laws of God, nature, and society.

The spirit of the anti-Christ is the expression of all humanity as a reflection of the destructive, evil, and deceiving nature of Satan. When Christ is not in people's lives, they will do only evil and follow the devil as we read in John 8:44: "Ye are of your father the devil and his will you will do."

Throughout the church age, theologians have speculated on the identity of the anti-Christ. The problem with these speculations is that they are always tentative and based on limited perspectives. What we are sure of from Scripture is that Satan must prepare someone in every generation to fill the role and to wear the crown of Satan. Therefore, we should not be surprised at the list of potential candidates these past twenty-one centuries.

For this terminal generation, it is most reasonable to assume that the unveiling of the anti-Christ following the rapture of the church is fast approaching. The blessing for the saved is that they will never see the anti-Christ revealed; the curse for the lost is that they will see his revealing (2 Thessalonians 2:1–12).

According to Scripture, the anti-Christ will be a Gentile rising to power out of the European nations. Jesus Christ is the only begotten Son of God; the word *only in* Greek means *"unique"*; the anti-Christ prepared, possessed, and empowered by Satan will be fulfilled by a person, not a fallen angel or demon. The anti-Christ will have all the characteristics of his identity revealed in Bible prophecy.

1. He will rise to power in the last days following the rapture (Daniel 8:19, 23).
2. He will rule the world (Revelation 13:7).
3. His headquarters will initially be in Rome (Revelation 17:8–9).
4. He will be intelligent and persuasive (Daniel 7:20).
5. He will rule by international consent (Revelation 17:12–13).

6. He will rule by deception (Daniel 8:24–25).
7. He will control the global economy (Revelation 13:16–17).
8. He will make a peace agreement/treaty with Israel for three and a half years (Daniel 9:27).
9. He will break the treaty and invade Israel (Daniel 9:26).
10. He will be wounded in the arm and eye and recover in a counterfeit resurrection (Zechariah 11:17).
11. He will claim to be God (2 Thessalonians 2:4).

In verses 3 and 4, John saw a red horse, peace was taken from earth, and worldwide anarchy took hold. Jesus foretold this in His Olivet Discourse to the disciples (Matthew 24:4–15); Jesus said there would be a false Christ in the last days and war, rumors of war, famines, pestilences, earthquakes, martyrs, and a false prophet we will see introduced in the later chapters of Revelation.

In verses 5 and 6, John saw a black horse with the rider that brought death by famine and carried scales. Famine is always present in times of conflict; food will be scarce, and the scales reveal that what food is available will be carefully rationed. A *denarius, a Roman penny,* was a day's wage and would purchase in Jesus' day eight measures of wheat and twenty-four measures of barley. In other words, at the time of the anti-Christ, money will have only one-eighth of its normal purchasing power; it will buy one measure of wheat and three of barley.

It is interesting to note the phrase, "hurt not the oil or the wine." What an ironic twist in this terrible situation! Luxury items will still be available for the wealthy. During the Great Depression, which lasted from 1929 to 1939, many Americans stood in bread lines (the wheat and barley), waited at soup kitchens, or simply died of starvation while the wealthy lived lives of luxury. This ghastly picture of starvation is captured for us in Lamentations 2:11–12, 19:20, 4:3, 4:5–7, 20, and Ezekiel 5:10. During the days of the Babylonian siege of Jerusalem in 586 BC and the Roman siege of Jerusalem in AD 70, the prophets recorded starvation and cannibalism in the city and people scavenging through the dung in the streets for morsels of grain.

In verse 7 and 8, John saw a pale horse whose rider was death and hell; spiritual death, physical death, torture, pain, and suffering. In this, we witness Satan's rule of his anti-Christ. Death will fall upon **1.75 billion humans, a quarter of the world's population of 7 billion in the *terminal generation*.** The deaths will be the result of wars, anarchy, food riots, starvation, and beasts of the earth. These beasts are not lions, tigers and bears but *rats!* Rats have been responsible for the deaths of more people that all wars combined. Rats carry over thirty-five diseases, and their fleas carry the bubonic plague, which was responsible for the death of a third of Europeans in the fourteenth century. Rats also carry typhus, which has killed over 200 million. Dead bodies during this seal judgment will litter the streets and alleys everywhere for lack of people or places to bury them.

In verses 9 through 11, the cry of the martyred during the tribulation was heard as never before. These martyrs died for the Word of God, and it is important to note that a million will accept Jesus Christ as their Savior during the tribulation. To accept Christ during the reign of the anti-Christ will cost them their lives, and in Revelation 6:9–11, they cry out to God for justice. These are three great theological implications in this passage.

1. It refutes the doctrine of "soul sleep"; these martyrs are in heaven not because of the rapture of the church or the first resurrection of the dead in Revelation 20:5–6, but are alive, awake, conscious, and have memories and bodies.
2. It refutes the doctrine of only one general resurrection. These souls of the tribulation martyrs have not yet received their glorified bodies and will not until the first resurrection of the dead with the bodies of the righteous Old Testament saints.
3. It reveals an intermediate body, similar to Christ following His resurrection on Easter before going to the Father to sprinkle His blood on the mercy seat in heaven and setting the captives free in paradise. We know these martyrs have a body in Scripture to place a robe on; they are not disembodied spirits but simply have not yet received their glorified bodies.

In verses 12 through 17, the opening of the sixth seal brings us to the beginning of the last half of the great tribulation of 1,260 days. The greatest earthquake ever will shift the continental plates, and the smoke resulting from this calamity will blot out the sunlight (Joel 2:30–32).

The greatest cosmic occurrence in history will take place as prophesied in Isaiah 34:4–5. Hal Lindsey wrote that this may be the result of a nuclear war that shakes the world's foundations due to the wording and description given by the prophet of the power and the rolling away like a scroll (Zechariah 14:12, 2; Peter 3:10–11). Zechariah 14:12 describes the flesh melting off a skeleton in a moment, eyes dissolving in their sockets, and the tongue dissolving in the mouth due to the fervent heat released by this judgment.

It is interesting that as we study creation and God's divine location and order of the planets in our solar system, we find that Earth is positioned perfectly from the sun for warmth, light, and life. God gave Jupiter a mass, location, and orbit that allows it to protect Earth from asteroids and meteors.

Great, mighty, and rich people prayed, but not for salvation. They didn't pray to God but to created things just as Romans 1:18–32 states. They prayed to be hidden from the wrath of the Lamb. What a paradox! Lambs are not normally associated with wrath. They had fled Christ; they had not sought Him.

Who shall be able to stand against the judgments of God? No one!

An Intermission to Seal and Save: Revelation 7

1. The intervention of God by the command of God—7:1–3
2. The sealing of the 144,000 of Israel—7:4–8
3. The vision of the Gentiles saved during the tribulation—7:9–17

In Revelation 6, we read about the opening of the first six seals of the tribulation judgment by Jesus Christ, the revealing of the anti-Christ, and the death and destruction of a quarter of the world's population by famine, pestilence, earthquakes, cosmic disturbances, and death. God was judging sinful humanity, and the days of Satan's reign as the prince and the power of the air of this world were numbered (Daniel 9:27; Revelation 20:10).

In the Bible, Satan is often referred to as the prince and the power of the air. In Matthew 12:29, the Pharisees ascribed this blasphemous title to Jesus Christ for resurrecting Lazarus. The Pharisees used the word *Beelzebub,* "*Lord of the flies*" or "*Prince of devils.*" John 12:31 contains Jesus' warning of the prince of this present world who will be cast out. Paul the apostle wrote in Ephesians 2:2, "Wherein in time past ye walked according to the course of this world, according to the prince of the power of the air, the spirit than now worketh in the children of disobedience."

Jesus Christ rebuked the seventy disciples when they returned from their ministry for rejoicing in being able to cast out demons in Jesus' name. In Luke 10:17–20, Jesus told them,

> I beheld Satan as lightning fall from heaven. Behold I give unto you power to tread on serpents and scorpions, and over all the power of the enemy; and nothing shall by any means hurt you. Notwithstanding in this rejoice not, that the spirits are subject unto you; but rather rejoice, because your names are written in heaven.

Satan's authority over the world is restricted by God (Job 1:12, 2:6), but it is still far reaching and encompasses all the powers of darkness (Ephesians 6:10–12; 2 Corinthians 10:3–6). God the Father, Son, and Holy Spirit have no equal; Satan, the anti-Christ, and the false prophet are not their opposites, but they do form an unholy trinity of Satan's reign in the world and this terminal generation.

There is an important matter to consider about the span and duration of Satan's rule as the prince and power of the air; in Luke's record of the temptation of Christ in the wilderness, Satan tempted Jesus to prove He was indeed the Son of God by turning stones into bread. Jesus rebuked Satan with the Word of God from Deuteronomy 8:3. Satan offered Jesus the kingdoms of the world if He would worship Satan. Jesus rebuked

Satan again with the Word of God from Deuteronomy 6:13. Satan tempted Jesus to prove Himself by tempting God's protection over Jesus by using the Word of God. Jesus rebuked Satan again with Scripture from Deuteronomy 10:20, telling Satan that he should not tempt the Lord thy God. Satan departed from Him for a season.

Satan tried to tempt Jesus with a short cut to the kingdom and a way to avoid suffering on the cross. In this, we thank God for Jesus' obedience; He endured the shame of the cross for the sake of our souls. In Revelation, we must remember that Satan is powerful but God is omnipotent and sovereign over all things.

Revelation 7 is an interlude, an intermission chapter between the seal judgments and the coming trumpet judgments of chapter 8. In chapter 7, we see God's mercy (Psalm 136:1–3), His will (2 Peter 3:9), and His power (Matthew 28:18).

Verse 1 deals with the restraining power of God over Satan. (See Daniel 7:2 and Ephesians 2:2 for the interpretation of this verse.) Remember that no passage of Scripture admits of any private interpretation (2 Peter 1:19–21) and that we must compare Scripture to Scripture to understand prophecy and rightly divide the Word of God (2 Timothy 2:15). The wind bound by the four angels of God was the spirit of unrest that Satan, the prince and the power of the air in this present world, blows over the sea of humanity.

Verses 1 and 3 of this chapter foreshadow the trumpet judgments to come after the sealing of the 144,000 Jewish virgin males selected from the twelve tribes of Jacob/Israel. The command of God in verse 3 was accomplished through the strength and obedience of a mighty angel commanding other angels that held the four winds. We must remember that God controls the weather on earth, including rains and drought. God controls the rotation of the earth and the course of the stars and planets. (See Genesis 7:6–12, 8:1 on the judgment of the worldwide flood of Noah's days. See Isaiah 38:3–8 on the setting of the sun, or better, the earth rotating backward and the shadow retreating. See 1 Kings 18:1; God says He will send the rain, and Elijah will once again be used by God in Revelation 11:3–7.)

The winds of unrest were restrained to preserve the earth, the sea, and the trees until the 144,000 witnesses of the gospel of Christ were set apart to evangelize the world.

In verses 2 and 3, we see the introduction of a fifth angel who commanded the other four that had power over the earth to judge. This mighty angel came from the eastern quarter, from which God's glory is manifest every twenty-four hours with the rising of the sun, the imminent rise of Jesus Christ for the church, and the Second Advent of Christ following the seven years of tribulation upon the earth. At that time, Jesus will ascend and recover the throne of King David as rightful Heir and rule as King of Kings and Lord of Lords in His millennial reign. Thy kingdom come, Jesus, and thy will be done! (Matthew 6:9–13).

The mighty angel is not to be confused with Jesus; He is on the throne in heaven and conducting the tribulation judgments by His authority, the title deed to the earth that the scroll represents.

This angel was carrying the seal of the Living God, which spoke of the power, preservation, and protection of God. Seals were applied many times in the Old and the New Testaments; see Ezekiel 8:1–6, about the sealing of the righteous with a mark or seal on their foreheads. Ephesians 1:13–14 deals with the sealing of the Holy Spirit on all born-again believers in Jesus Christ. Likewise, a seal was set upon Satan in Revelation 20:3 to bind him for a thousand years in the bottomless pit, the abyss, hell, during Christ's millennial reign on earth following the great tribulation . It was not the location or the chains that bound Satan; it was the seal of the Living God that prevented his escape for 1,000 years. Interesting point? If Satan in his evil nature will be bound by God away from the righteous, and Satan is certainly the most powerful created being, how much more secure are the sealed saints of God in their salvation? Romans 8:38–39 declares that neither life nor death, angels, or principalities nor any other creature can separate us from the love of God in Christ Jesus.

The command of the Lord was to delay the judgments on earth and sinful humanity until the 144,000 servants of God were sealed in their foreheads by the mark of the Living God.

Verses 4 through 8 deal with the sealing of the 144,000. It should be no wonder that the seal of the Living God is a seal of protection that guarantees that the will of God will be fulfilled according to His prophetic words. Throughout Scripture, God preserved His saints from natural and supernatural disasters and judgments; examples of this in the Old and New Testaments are numerous. Noah and his family were saved from the flood; that story is one of the most fascinating narratives in the early pages of the Bible. God chose Noah for his righteousness and submissive obedience; this reflected God's discernment. He chose Noah to preach His warnings to the mass of humanity, which could have numbered 18 million then, and Noah preached about the flood for 120 years. Longsuffering God was not willing to let anyone perish; He wanted all to repent, but the multitudes laughed at Noah as though he were a madman.

God had Noah provision the ark, and God called the animals to the ark, showing His love for all His creation and His preservation of seed to replenish the earth. The ark was a typology of Jesus Christ in that it had no sail, oars, or rudder. It had only one door and one window and was designed for one trip. This typology is the atonement sacrifice of Jesus Christ, the ark of our salvation who carries us safely through the storm and judgment upon the unrighteous.

Before the rain fell, God called Noah, his wife, his sons, and his sons' wives into the ark to preserve the family. What a wonderful example of our safety in Jesus Christ, secure in the love of God, entering through the door of faith, and seeing through the one window the light of the world, Jesus Christ. The ark was not steered by Noah but moved by the breath and sovereign will of God until it came to rest when the waters abated.

Many today believe they must hang onto their salvation or lose it. God did not tell Noah to drive eight nails on the outside of the ark and then hang on until the rain stopped and the waters abated. The only nails of our salvation were driven into the hands and feet of Jesus Christ on a Roman cross two thousand years ago. God preserved, spared, and separated the Hebrew nation from the ten plagues He sent on Pharaoh and the Egyptians to secure the Hebrew children's release from 400 years of slavery and captivity as promised prophetically to Abraham in Genesis 15:13–14.

God then preserved 1.5 million Hebrews during the forty years they wandered the wilderness. He providing them manna, quail, and water. Their shoes and clothes never wore out. God preserving, providing, protecting, leading, and saving souls is God at His best!

God spared the three Hebrew boys tossed into the fiery furnace by the guards of King Nebuchadnezzar, and He sent His Son, the *preincarnate Christ,* to comfort them through the fire as testimony of God's great preserving power and mercy. Daniel was preserved through the night in the den of lions, and God spared 276 souls alive with the apostle Paul during his shipwreck on the isle of Melita.

John heard the number of those sealed as 144,000, and he understood that 12,000 were selected from each of the twelve tribes of Jacob's sons, Israel. Once again, we witness the truth and accuracy of God's Word and prophecy to Abraham in Genesis 12:3: "Through you all the nations of the earth shall be blessed." This is the prophecy to Jacob in Genesis 35:10 when Jacob's name was changed by God to Israel. Additionally, the twelve tribes of Israel are given in Revelation 7, but note must be taken when comparing the Old Testament Scriptures of the names that Dan and Ephraim are two sons not mentioned in the sealing of the 144,000. Dan and Ephraim were guilty of perverting worship to God, of moving the appointed place of worship from Jerusalem to the city of Dan, of idolatry, and of oppression of Judah. God's vessels for service must be consecrated for use, and Dan and Ephraim lost their places because of sin. Their places among the 144,000 were taken by Levi and Manasseh, the sons of Joseph.

The number 144,000 reflects the mercy of God in the abundance of the evangelist being sent into the world during the tribulation as compared to the 35,000 missionaries from all denominations in mission fields today.

Keep in mind why. Matthew 24:14 tells us, "This gospel of the kingdom shall be preached in all the world, for a witness unto all nations." This outreach ministry during the darkest days of the tribulation will extend to Jews and the Gentiles alike, and then the end shall come.

Note that Paul the apostle stated he was the apostle born out of time, not referring to his late arrival on the road to Damascus but to his early arrival, before the calling of the 144,000. In a proper translation, Paul used the phrase *out of time* to mean *"premature birth."* The miracle that God worked on the road to Damascus with Paul almost 2,000 years ago is the same call of God upon the 144,000 to share the gospel of Christ to a lost, dying, and **terminal generation in the twenty-first century.** In his commentary on Revelation, Dr. J. D. Pentecost had some excellent insight worthy of reading on this statement of Paul concerning being born out of time.

We will see these 144,000 again in Revelation. In Revelation 11, during the first three and a half years of the tribulation, God will use His two witnesses at the Western Wall in Jerusalem, the Wailing Wall, to proclaim the gospel of Christ to the Jews and the world. At the end of the 1,260 days or three and a half years of the two witnesses' ministry, the anti-Christ will have these two witnesses, Elijah and Moses, slain. Their bodies will lie in the streets of Jerusalem for three days as the world empires rejoice in their death and give gifts to each other in celebration like an unholy Christmas. Then to the world's horror, God will resurrect and recall the two witnesses to heaven. Immediately after this, God will call the 144,000 witnesses of chapter 7 as detailed in Revelation 14:1–5. Note that because of the seal of the Living God on the foreheads of these 144,000, all 144,000 will preach, live, and survive during their ministry on earth during the tribulation period, and none will be lost. God has never lost a sealed, saved saint! Amen.

All of the 144,000 were from the twelve tribes of Israel, all were males, all were virgins, and they all followed Jesus Christ (Revelation 14:1–5).

In verse 1 of Revelation 7 and in verse 9 again, we read the familiar statement, *meta tauta, "after this";* a change of scene occurred, and John saw in verse 9 a great multitude of people saved during the tribulation and great tribulation period comprising all nations and peoples. They were standing before the throne of Christ, *the bema seat,* clothed in white robes of righteousness and holding palm leaves. This is an antitype of Christ's entry into Jerusalem 2,000 years ago on His triumphal entry preceding His passion.

The cry was the same as the cries of the multitude in Jerusalem 2,000 years ago: "Salvation to our God, and to the Lamb, Hosanna." *Hosanna* translates as "save us now." Less than a week later, the multitude rejected Christ and cried out to crucify Him, saying that they had no king but Caesar, saying that His blood should be upon them and their children. How many today reject the Messiah, not realizing their salvation is slipping away in these last, late days of the **terminal generation?**

When the angels, the angelic creatures, and the elders heard the song of the redeemed, they fell down and worshipped God. Angels praise God when people are saved because they know the terrors of hell, they know Christ died for humanity, and they know God saving a soul is God at His best!

In verse 13, John was asked who the people in white robes were. John answered that he didn't know. The answer was given to John and us today: "These are the ones saved during the Great Tribulation, washing their robes in the blood of the Lamb." This passage reminds me of that great old hymn, "There is a fountain filled with blood, drawn from Emmanuel's veins, washing away all their guilty stains." How sad it is today that new translations of the Bible have removed so many of its precious words. Society today finds the word *blood* offensive, the *virgin birth* of Christ as unbelievable science, the final destination of *hell* for the unrepentant sinner as too graphic, and the only path of salvation by faith alone, by Christ alone, by grace alone, as too narrow minded. The *road to apostasy is paved with poor Bible translations.*

The goodness of heaven is reflected in the saints who stand before the throne of God and serve God; God dwells among them (Revelation 21:3).

The promise, the provision, and the protection of God from the Word of God is that we will not hunger or thirst or be scorched by the sun, that Christ will feed us and lead us to fountains of living water and wipe away our tears.

I wonder if these saints have the same regret as many of us today for the years we have wasted by not having received Jesus Christ as our Savior sooner in life, or having not served faithfully in our Christian life sooner, or having suffered or caused needless suffering because of our meager service to Christ.

Though God has not called all to be preachers, pastors, teachers, or missionaries, He has called all of us to the ministry of reconciliation. We are all called to tell others about Jesus Christ, to share the gospel good news of Jesus Christ's life, death, burial, and resurrection, and to invite people to receive Jesus Christ as their Savior.

Part V

The Seal Judgments Resumed, the Seventh Seal, and the Trumpet Judgments: Revelation Chapters 8–9

1. Silence in heaven—8:1
2. The seven angels with seven trumpets—8:2–6
3. The first trumpet judgment—8:7
4. The second trumpet judgment—8:8–9
5. The third trumpet judgment—8:10–11
6. The fourth trumpet judgment: woe, woe, woe—8:12–13
7. The firth trumpet judgment and the first woe, demonic affliction—9:1–12
8. The sixth trumpet judgment—9:13–21

In Revelation 7, we observed the mercy, will, and power of God in the interlude that chapter 7 represents with the sealing of the 144,000 and the saved of the tribulation period who accepted Christ as their Savior. The angels, the twenty-four elders, and the saints before the throne of God in heaven worshipped and praised the Lord. In the closing verses of chapter 7, we read about the provision, promises, and protection of God for His saints. We will read about the longsuffering patience of God in chapter 8 in the silence in heaven for thirty minutes as Scripture moves forward prophetically into the trumpet judgments of the **terminal generation.**

Revelation has often been subtitled "From Creation to Re-Creation," and in chapter 8, we see God deconstructing His creation in the trumpet judgments. We will also note the inerrancy of Scripture, and the trumpet judgments carry us back to Numbers 10:1–10, when God instructed Moses to fashion two trumpets of silver that would assemble the twelve tribes around the wilderness tabernacle and to sound the alarm to the tribes when danger was approaching. The trumpets of Revelation serve similarly to call the assembly, the church, together. The trumpet blast also calls the New Testament saints together in the rapture of the church; the trumpet is also for the assembling of God's chosen people: Israel, Judah, Jerusalem, the nation of Israel, and the remnant. Finally, the trumpets are to sound an alarm and warning of things to come and to repent and prepare to meet God.

This chapter begins with the conjunction *and*, which tells us this is a continuation of the tribulation period. The pronoun *His* refers to Jesus

Christ as the only one worthy to open the final seal judgment upon the earth and sinful humanity with the trumpet judgments.

In verse 1, we also learn that there will be silence in heaven for about half an hour. This is the only time when there was silence in heaven; angels will not sing, and no one will move.

During the sixth seal judgment, humanity will weaken for the first time in the tribulation, and a merciful and patient God will listen and wait for the prayers of repentance because God takes no pleasure in the death of the wicked (Ezekiel 33:11), but it will be to no avail.

The duration of the silence was thirty minutes; the number 30 in the Bible is often associated with mourning. Aaron, the brother of Moses, in Numbers 20:29 and Moses in Deuteronomy 34:8 mourned over sin and death.

In verses 2 through 6, Jesus Christ interceded for us before the throne of God. The seven angels standing before God received seven trumpets that came out of the sixth seal.

Another angel came to stand at the golden altar with a golden censer filled with much incense and offered it before God with the prayers of the saints in verses 3 and 4. This passage carries us back to Leviticus 16:12, in which the high priest offered the atonement blood sacrifice upon the mercy seat. This signifies that Jesus Christ is our great High Priest who presented His blood on heaven's mercy seat and sacrificed Himself on the altar of the cross for humanity's sins. Christ alone is therefore worthy to judge or to pardon.

Jesus' qualifications as the only one worthy to offer Himself as the sacrifice for humanity's sins as our great High Priest and Redeemer are fourfold.

1. Jesus Christ was not under the calamity of sin and had no sin nature (2 Corinthians 5:21).
2. Jesus was our near-kinsman Redeemer with full authority to redeem humanity. Jesus Christ was all God and all man in His

*hypostatic **union*** of God and humanity at His *incarnation* (John 1:14).

3. Jesus paid the full redemption price for our sins and souls (John 2:2).
4. Jesus was qualified and acceptable to God the Father as the only sacrifice for our sins, transgressions, and iniquities (John 1:29, 3:16).

When the angel took the censer and filled it with fire (the purification foreshadowed in Isaiah 6:6–7) from the altar of God and cast it to earth, there were voices, thundering, lightning, and an earthquake. This is consistent with God's judgment and presence to Moses on Mount Sinai in the giving of the Ten Commandments, and with Elijah the prophet at the mouth of the cave in 1 Kings 19:8–12.

The seven angels were standing as soldiers at rapt attention awaiting the Lord's orders and commands; they were prepared to sound their trumpets. The angels stood before God, as we will in the last days. We must prepare ourselves for salvation, service, and ministry the Lord God has appointed for us. We prepare by

- following the leading of the Holy Spirit (Luke 4:1),
- studying the Word to show ourselves approved unto the Lord (2 Timothy 2:15),
- waiting patiently for the Lord (Psalm 37:7),
- being obedient to God's commands (John 15:10–14),
- embracing God's promises (Philippians 4:13, 19),
- embracing the gifts the Holy Spirit gives us in this life (Ephesians 4:11–12), and
- living Spirit-filled lives and bringing forth fruit of the Spirit to a lost and dying world (Ephesians 5:18–20; Galatians 5:22–23).

In verse 7, the first trumpet judgment sounded, and hail and fire mingled with blood were cast upon the earth, resulting in the destruction of a third of all trees and grass. Plant life, the first part of creation (Genesis 1:11–12), was the first to be destroyed. This will result in an unparalleled ecological disaster. The increase in temperature will cause a dust-bowl effect similar to the dust storms across the Southwestern United States in the 1930s, and the oxygen content of the world will be depleted by 33 percent.

When look back at God's judgments upon Egypt, Pharaoh, and the Egyptians in Exodus 9:23–25 for enslaving God's people, we see that God does not change. Satan will focus his attention on Israel, and his hatred will intensify. The tribulation period is referred to by the prophets and by Jesus Christ as the great tribulation, the great and terrible day of the Lord, and the *time of Jacob's trouble.*

In verses 8 and 9, the second trumpet judgment was sounded. Dr. Herman Hoyt wrote that the mountain of fire in these verses might refer to a meteor that will turn a third of saltwater to blood; this will encompass all the world's oceans and great seas. In Exodus 7:19, God used water turned to blood as a judgment upon Egypt. The result of this judgment will be that a third of sea life, including plants, plankton, fish, and mammals, will die.

Additionally, a third of all the ships on the sea that day will be destroyed, resulting in an ecological and economic disaster of apocalyptic proportions. Oil tankers, fishing factories, and cruise ships will sink. Famine will result from the collapse of coastal nations and cities.

God gave us the salt sea to act as a giant purifier; all fresh water and waste run to the oceans and seas and is purified by the salt. When saltwater evaporates, it is returned over the land in the form of pure rain, snow, and ice.

In verses 10 and 11, the third trumpet sounded the next judgment; Wormwood, a great star, fell and poisoned a third of all fresh water. Many species of wormwood grow in Palestine, and they have a strong, bitter taste. Wormwood is mentioned nine times in the Bible and is always associated with judgment. You can learn more about wormwood by googling it; astronomers are tracking a star in this millennium that was unknown to us before the advent of space telescopes. The star being tracked is Wormwood*!*

In verses 12 and 13, the fourth trumpet judgment sounded, and a third of the sun and moon were affected; there was no light for a third of the day. The Lord may have had this judgment in mind when He spoke the words of the Olivet Discourse in Matthew 24:22: "Except those days be shortened, there shall no flesh be saved, but for the elects sake those days shall be shortened." Reference verses of forewarning are in Luke 21:25 and Amos 8:9. Note that God created the sun, the moon, and the stars on the fourth day (Genesis 1:14–16), and they were for signs, season, days, and years.

The darkness will be terrifying and absolute for eight hours per day (Exodus 10:21–23). This darkness will be felt, and no one will move during this time. Power-generating stations, hydroelectric power plants, and nuclear power plants need cooling water to operate, and no doubt their intake pipes will be plugged by syrupy, bloody water, dead fish, and animals from the second and third trumpet judgments. And who will operate these power stations? The **1.75 billion people who will** have died because of the judgments thus far in the tribulation period won't be able to.

The flying angel in verse 13 is best translated as an eagle. Some may disagree, but we will see this eagle again, a crying voice without a trumpet, just a message for sinful humanity to repent. Woe, woe, woe to the inhabitants of earth!

Verse 13 is a separation between the two periods of the tribulation. This verse is significant in that it separates the first three and a half years from the final three and a half years of the great tribulation. The last three trumpets to follow are terrifying spiritual attacks by Satan and the demons released from hell. Once again, remember that all the judgments are not in chronological order; some overlap these epic periods.

God's Judgment Forewarning in the Ages Past and the Age to Come in Our Terminal Generation

In Joel 2:30–31, we read, "I will show wonders in the heavens and in the earth, blood and fire and pillars of smoke. The sun shall be turned into darkness, and the moon into blood, before the great and terrible day of the LORD to come."

In 2 Peter 3:9, we read, "The Lord is not slack concerning his promise, as some men count slackness, but is longsuffering to us-ward, and not willing that any should perish, but that all should come to repentance."

God issued His warnings prior to His judgments in Scripture and prophecy.

1. God warned Adam he would die if he ate from the Tree of Knowledge of Good and Evil. Death did not overtake Adam for 930 years, but during those years, he labored under the curse of sin, worked by the sweat of his brow, and experienced loss and heartache from the crushing burden of sin and regret.

2. God warned Pharaoh to let his people leave Egypt. Because of Pharaoh's pride and sinful rebellion against Moses, Aaron, and the nation of Israel, ten plagues fell on Egypt and Pharaoh's house and led to the destruction of Egypt's mighty army in the Red Sea and the demise of the Egyptian Empire.

3. God warned Israel of its sins of idolatry, adultery, immorality, oppression of the poor and strangers, and perverting justice. Israel, Judah, and Jerusalem went into Assyrian and Babylonian captivity.

4. Through the voices of the prophets Isaiah, Jeremiah, Ezekiel, and Daniel and the minor prophets, God repeatedly warned Jews and Gentiles of His coming judgment in the final days against sin.

5. Jesus Christ wept over Jerusalem for its rejection of the kingdom of God and the Messiah. Christ announced the coming judgment and dispersion of the nation. This judgment fell upon Jerusalem and Israel in AD 70, when Titus destroyed the city and the temple, not leaving one stone on top of another.

6. In the Olivet Discourse, Jesus warned the Gentile nations that Israel would be brought back to the land as a nation again preceding the last days, that the Hebrew language would be revived, and that the Gentile world powers would be subdued. The *trigger point* for this fulfillment was May 14, 1948, when Israel became a sovereign

nation again, flying the flag with the Star of David. In Matthew 24:32–34, we read,

> Now learn the parable of the fig tree; When his branch is yet tender, and putteth forth leaves, know that summer is nigh [the branch is Jesus Christ: Zechariah 3:8], so likewise ye, when ye shall see all these things, know that it is near, even at the doors. Verily I say unto you, this generation shall not pass away, till all these things be fulfilled.

This is but one of the greatest scriptural evidences of the **terminal generation.** We are the **terminal generation** that will be alive at the rapture of the church. This is the next great cataclysmic event facing humanity and the world as we know it. Our generation and life is about to change forever!

"And There Will Be Signs in the Heavens"

Blood-red lunar eclipses and solar eclipses will occur on God's holy days in 2014–2015.

> Astonishing as it seems, four lunar eclipses will occur on God's annual Holy Days during Passover and Sukkot in the years 2014 and 2015, and two solar eclipses on Nisan 1 and the Feast of Trumpets! These are exceptionally rare occurrences, especially when compared to God's Holy Days! What is the prophetic significance? It is time to wake up and take heed of these ominous, fateful warnings from heaven![3]

According to the Jewish calendar, 2014 is a sabbatical year. A new sabbatical cycle began September 29, 2008; therefore, 2015 will also be a sabbatical year. But most amazing of all, in the years 2014 and 2015, there will also be two solar eclipses and four lunar eclipses, all of them occurring on Jewish

---

3   William F. Dankenbring

holy days. The lunar eclipses break down as follows: Passover on April 15, 2014; the Feast of Tabernacles on October 8, 2014; Passover on April 4, 2015; and the Feast of Tabernacles on September 28, 2015. The two solar eclipses connected with God's holy days in 2014–2015 occur on March 20, 2015, and September 13, 2015.

The Hebrew New Year occurred on Nisan 1, according to Scriptures (Exodus 12:1–2). On the anniversary of this date one year later, Moses raised up the Tabernacle of God, inaugurated it, and the glory of God descended from heaven (Exodus 40:17, 34).

The real shocker is that this pattern of eclipses to fall on both the Passover and Sukkot two years in a row and for solar eclipses to occur on important holy days in the same year, 2015, is extremely rare. This intriguing and incredible discovery came from Mark Biltz, the pastor of El Shaddai Ministries in Bonner Lake, Washington. Biltz was intrigued with the statement in the Scriptures that connects the second coming of the Messiah with "signs and wonders in the heavens" and particularly the sign that the sun will be turned to darkness and the moon to blood before the return of Christ. He went to NASA's website to see if there were any significant eclipses of the sun or moon during the next five years. To his surprise, he discovered four lunar eclipses in the sabbatical year 2014–2015 and was intrigued by the fact that they were to occur on God's annual holy days.

Writing about this amazing discovery in the May 2008 issue of *Prophecy in the News,* J. R. Church declared, "This is most unusual; it is a rare occurrence for four lunar cycles on successive Passovers and the Feast of Tabernacles [Sukkot] observances. It will not happen again for several centuries."

Church stated in his letter accompanying the magazine article,

> Four lunar eclipses occurring on the Feast of Tabernacles and the Passover in two successive years are phenomenal. But added to them two solar eclipses on the two days that open the Jewish year, Adar 29, and Nisan 1, just two weeks before the Passover and Tishri (Rosh Hashannah)

is uncanny. On each of these six Jewish holy days, the sun will be darkened and the moon will not give light. Will this happen again in the twenty-first century? No. Did it happen in the twentieth century? Yes, in 1949 and 1950, the year following Israel's statehood and in 1967–1968, the year Jerusalem was liberated in the Six-Day War. Before that, you have to go back to 1493 for four consecutive lunar eclipses on Passover and the Feast of Tabernacles. (May 2008 Letter)

God is telling us that something very spectacular and special from Scripture. Skeptics and scoffers will denounce the discovery as mere coincidence, but the prophet Daniel informed us, "Many shall be purified, made white, and refined. But the wicked shall do wickedly, and none of the wicked will understand, but the wise will understand" (Daniel 12:10). In addition, Peter warned, "Scoffers will come in the last days, walking according to their own lust, and saying, 'where is the promise of his coming?' For since the fathers fell asleep, all things continue as they were from the beginning of creation" (2 Peter 3:3–4).

Biltz believes that these phenomenal solar eclipses signify God could begin judging the Gentile nations. Solar eclipses are designed for the Gentile nations, whereas lunar eclipses are designed for Israel. These eclipses could be a warning from God to a wayward world.

Biltz focused on the precise times of the solar and lunar eclipses, sometimes called "blood moons," by logging onto NASA's website on eclipses. He noticed a rare phenomenon of four consecutive total lunar eclipses, a *tetrad*. During this century, tetrads will occur at least six times, but the only string of four consecutive blood moons coinciding with God's holy days on Passover and the Feast of Tabernacles occurs only in the years 2014 and 2015 based on today's Gregorian calendar. It is noteworthy that in the twentieth century, the only successive blood moons coinciding with the feast occurred in 1967–1968, the year the Jews liberated Jerusalem from the control of the surrounding Arab nations. He also noted the only other such combination of eclipses in the twentieth century took place in

1949–1950, the year following the Jewish state's hard-fought civil war of independence, when Israel became a nation again.

Signs in the Heavens

Why did God create stars? We find one answer in Genesis 1:14: "And God said, Let there be lights in the expanse of the sky to separate the day from the night, and let them serve as *signs* to mark seasons and days and years." The word for *sign* in Hebrew is *owth, which* means a signal, flag, beacon, monument, omen, prodigy, evidence, and so on. The word for *seasons* in Hebrew is *moadim, which* means "festivals," literally translated as "appointed times."

Thus, the heavenly bodies, the periodic return of comets, meteor showers, and eclipses can be heavenly signs in biblical terms. Jesus spoke of such signs occurring before His return. When such signs occur on a *moad or a moadim, a* festival of God, it is especially significant. These are not mere speculations; the apostle Paul wrote,

> We have a more sure word of prophecy; whereunto ye do well that ye take heed, as unto a light that shineth in a dark place, until the day dawn, and the day star arise in your hearts. Knowing this first, that no prophecy of scripture is of any private interpretation. For prophecy came not in old time by the will of man, but holy men of God spake as they were moved by the Holy Spirit. (2 Peter 1:19–21)

Because prophecy is an integral part of the Word of God, it should not be taken lightly or disrespectfully; it is vital to our salvation. Over 28 percent of the Bible is prophetic, and 90 percent of the prophecy deals exclusively with the **last days of the terminal generation—who will be alive just before the return of Christ in awesome power and glory to deliver His people and save earth from annihilation. Paul commanded, "Never disdain prophetic revelations (1 Thessalonians 5:20), and do not scoff at those who prophesy."

What is the message for us today? Our generation, the generation of baby boomers, hippies, yuppies, generation X, and the millennials, will be the **terminal generation that will** see all these things come to pass! Some will witness the rapture of the church, and some will face the great tribulation for rejecting Jesus Christ as their personal Savior.

The Trumpet Judgments Continued: Revelation 9

In Revelation 8, we heard the sound of the first four trumpet judgments that resulted in a third of earth's vegetation being burned up, a third of the salt seas being turned to blood, a third of all fresh water being turned to blood, and the sun, moon, and stars being darkened for a third of each day. These judgments were followed by thirty minutes of silence in heaven as the Lord listened for prayers of repentance. Following the sounding of the fourth trumpet, an angel or eagle was heard flying through the heavens and crying out, "Woe, woe, woe" to the inhabitants of the earth by reason of the remaining three angels that were yet to sound. Remember that there are three heavens mentioned in the Bible: the first is our atmosphere, the second is outer space, and the third is God's abode.

In chapter 9, we read of the fifth and sixth trumpets sounding their judgments, and this occurs at the midpoint of the tribulation and results in a third of earth's remaining population perishing in a demonic attack unleashed from hell. The death toll is a staggering **1.75 billion.**

Before entering this section of the book, I want to lay some groundwork concerning hell so we are not confused in this difficult passage.

1. God created all things (Genesis 1:1), including hell, for a purpose. Hell was never created for human beings. In Matthew 25:41, we read, "Depart from me; ye cursed into everlasting fire, prepared for the devil and his angels." It is important when reading Revelation 9 to remember that the devil and his angels were the key characters in the fifth trumpet judgment.
2. Hell is the final destination for unrepentant sinners. Hell is mentioned 54 times in the Bible, and heaven is the destination

for the saints of God. Heaven is mentioned 584 times in the Old and New Testaments.

Hell in Hebrew is *sheol,* or the place of the unrighteous dead.[4] Hell in Greek is mentioned in three specific words that give us the location and description of hell. In *Strong's Concordance of the Bible, gheh-en-nah*[5] *is* the valley of Hinnon where the bodies of the dead were cast into the city's trash and animal carcasses and burned. Metaphorically, it is an earthly illustration of the characteristics of hell, a place of burning destruction, and Christ used the word as a warning to the unrepentant.

Hell is also defined in *Strong's* as Hades,[6] the place of torment of the unrighteous dead. It is important to note that both *Sheol and Hades* are getting fuller every day as testified by Isaiah the prophet in Isaiah 5:14–15. They contain the souls of the suffering and tormented unrighteous since the beginning of time. The other half of *Hades is called paradise* in the Bible, which Christ spoke of in His parable of the rich man and Lazarus in Luke 16:19–31. The rich man was suffering in Hades, and Lazarus was comforted in Abraham's bosom, paradise. Jesus Christ emptied paradise following His crucifixion and set the captives free (Psalm 68:18; Ephesians 4:8). Upon Jesus' death, the sins of humanity were no longer rolled back year after year by the atonement sacrifice in the temple but had been paid in full for all time, washed away by the blood of the Lamb, and these souls came into the presence of God the Father in heaven. Christ was the atonement sacrifice for sin (Hebrews 9:25–28; 1 John 2:2).

Hell as defined by *Strong's* is also *tartaros,*[7] the deepest abyss of Hades. It contains those incarcerated for eternal judgment, punishment, and suffering who have never repented of sin or accepted Jesus Christ as their personal Savior. It is *tartaros that* we see being opened in Revelation 9;

---

4   *Strong's Exhaustive Concordance of the Bible* 7585.

5   Ibid., 1067.

6   Ibid., 86.

7   Ibid., 5020.

Hades will not be opened until Revelation 20:13 for the judgment of the unrighteous dead before the great white throne of God.

The last three trumpet judgments in Revelation 9:1–12 are remarkably different from the previous four trumpet judgments; these last three are defined as woes; the woe judgments mark the deepest, darkest, and most painful of the great tribulation and are associated with the last three and a half years of the 1,260 days in Daniel's prophecies.

Revelation 9 is the most revealing section in the Bible concerning demonology. Other Scripture references on demonology are Isaiah 14:12–17, Ezekiel 28:1–19, and Luke 8:1–3, 26–39, and 16:19–31.

These bound demons are in the bottomless pit in verse 9:1. The words *bottomless pit* literally translate as the "shaft of the abyss," and God mentioned it no fewer than seven times in Revelation 9:1, 2, 11, 11:7, 17:8, and 20:1–3. By these scriptural descriptions, it is reasonable to identify the bottomless pit with the center of earth (Ephesians 4:8–10).

These demons are the fallen one-third of the angelic host that rebelled against God and followed Lucifer as detailed in Isaiah 14, Ezekiel 28, Revelation 12:9, and Luke 10:18. Some have identified this demonic horde as those in Genesis 6:1–2 that attempted sexual relations with human women that resulted in their immediate confinement to the abyss. The most likely reason God bound them in the abyss was their rebellion against God and their allegiance to Satan, which occurred during the first moments of Creation (Genesis 1:1–3).

Because of their evil power to corrupt and pervert, God in His mercy toward humanity bound them to keep them from corrupting the world. Jude 1, 6, and 7 and 1 Peter 2:4 attest to the fact that they are in the abyss, and it is there that Satan will be bound during Christ's millennial reign (Revelation 20:1–3).

The number of fallen angels in the world is beyond our ability to number, and likewise is the number of holy angels. Angels were created spiritual beings, and though they are not eternal or self-existent, they are immortal.

Christians cannot be possessed by demons since Christians have been sealed by the Holy Spirit of God, but sadly, Christians can submit themselves to demons and fall under their influence. Demons desire to possess and indwell human flesh, and this is witnessed today by the horrific crimes of passion and lust against humanity due to demonic possession. Demonic possession often manifests itself as mental illness, but the underlying cause in most cases is demonic control over the human mind and body.

Angels were created to be the servants and messengers of God, Christ, and the Holy Spirit and to protect and serve God's creation. Angels cannot procreate, and holy angels always bear the appearance of males. The Bible tells us clearly that Satan is not a little imp with long tail, horns, and a pitchfork. The greatest lie ever fostered upon humanity by Satan was, "I don't exist." The apostle Paul wrote in 2 Corinthians 11:14, "and no marvel, for Satan himself is transformed into an angel of light." Although hideous in character, sin often takes on the image of glitter, glamor, and gold. Read Ezekiel 28:13–19 for an accurate picture of Satan's appearance; he was created the most beautiful, powerful, and intelligent of God's angels and served as the praise and worship leader of the angelic choir in heaven until his rebellion and fall. "Oh Lucifer, how art thou fallen."

In Revelation 9:1, the person who released the demons from the abyss was Satan, not Jesus Christ. The star (one of the stars from Isaiah 14:12–14 written of by John as the star that fell from heaven) is Lucifer as recorded in Luke 10:18, Isaiah 14, and Ezekiel 28. Jesus Christ holds the keys to death and hell (Revelation 1:18), but He will allow Satan to hold the keys for a short season for a specific purpose. We must remember that God is not limited and has used unrighteous kings and people in past ages to fulfill His divine purposes. The Old Testament book of Habakkuk provides the wonderful narrative of God's divine judgment on Israel for its sins in this manner with the Chaldean invasion (Habakkuk 1:6).

Verses 3 and 4 inform us that out of the abyss came smoke and locusts on the earth and they had power as scorpions have power. This illustration of locusts and scorpions serves as an example of the demonic hordes being released from the abyss to afflict humanity in this trumpet woe judgment.

Notice the grace and mercy of God in this passage; God set limits on how far Satan could go, and although God is boundless in His nature, He also mercifully set boundaries on our adversary, Satan. This is revealed in the Old and New Testaments; God limited Satan on his actions against Job. God also set boundaries when the 144,000 were being sealed by binding the four winds of strife, not hurting the grass, trees, or any other green thing; He simply delayed the trumpet judgments for the sake of the evangelizing of the world. God's commands afflict only those who do not have the seal of the Living God on their foreheads. Satan turned his animosity toward Israel at that time in the tribulation, but God turned his animosity to sinful men.

As a side note concerning the perfect, justified wrath of God and for a unique insight into this aspect of God's nature, read the Old Testament book of Nahum. It is only three chapters long and deals with the destruction of Nineveh for its people's sin. Nineveh is called the bloody city in Nahum, but 150 years earlier, it was called the repentant city for having received the message of God from the prophet Jonah, and God spared the city.

Verses 5 and 6 reveal the limits God set upon Satan and his demonic army. For five months, demons could not kill people, but they could afflict them; the torment of this affliction was like a scorpion's sting—not deadly but painful, feverish, and debilitating. People sought death but did not find it. It sounds strange that people would attempt suicide but fail, but this was due to God's providence.

The demons looked like horses prepared for battle; they wore gold crowns (Nahum 3:1; Revelation 16:12), their faces looked like women's faces, and their teeth were like lions' teeth (Joel 1:6). They had breastplates of iron, and their wings made sounds like thundering chariots (Joel 2:5). They had scorpion-like tails and the power to hurt people.

Their king, mentioned in verse 11, was Satan, whose name was *death* and *destruction.* These two words are the Hebrew word *Abaddon,* but the Greek word is *Apollyon,* and one woe passed. It is interesting today how many have spiritualized and sensationalized the description of this demonic horde. These are demons, they have a king, they are not insects, and they are not conquering armies flying Black Hawk helicopters with rockets and bombs.

Application of These Verses to Our Lives Today

As the **terminal generation**, we are experiencing demonic activity in the world today similar to that experienced by Jesus Christ during His earthly ministry twenty-one centuries ago. Jesus frequently cast out demons from possessed persons; a young boy, a madman of Gadara who was possessed by a multitude of demons named *"Legion, for we are many." He cast out* seven demons from Mary Magdalene, among others. Today, society either refuses to believe in demons or actively seeks their presence. Demons are powerful, evil, fallen angels, and we must not seek to be in their presence or entertain activities that invite them into our lives. New agers refer to this as *"channeling spirits,"* which is just a way of requesting demonic possession over their bodies and minds. This occult practice is very popular and common among movie stars as is revealed in their profanity, brazen immorality, and excessive lifestyle of overindulgence in drugs, alcohol, and promiscuity.

We must stay away from any occult activity no matter how harmless or acceptable society deems it. Satan is actively recruiting followers in this **terminal generation** and will use the occult, astrology, horoscopes, palm readers, tarot cards, fortune-tellers, psychics, and TV and films to desensitize the masses to accept paranormal activity in preparation for the **last days and the release of the demonic hordes.** How many programs on television today encourage the search for UFOs, ancient aliens, ghosts, spirit activity, haunted houses, humans possessed by demons, vampires, werewolves, or Bigfoot? This is not a coincidence; this is Satan preparing for his attack on the world. Just as the Lord will reveal himself to those who seek Him (Revelation 3:20), Satan will also reveal himself to those who seek him. It is reported that 83 percent of those who believe they have seen a UFO, Bigfoot, or a ghost have been previously involved in occult activities.

Verses 13 through 19 deal with the sixth trumpet. The voice John the apostle heard was the voice of Jesus Christ, and the four horns of the altar are symbolic of the power of God. Christ commanded the sixth angel to loose the four angels that were bound in the Euphrates River at that time. These four evil angels will lead the invasion against Israel; their service to Satan will serve as a counterfeit, unholy, angelic gathering that will stand in contrast to the four living angelic creatures that praise God around the throne of heaven (Revelation 4:6–8).

The armies of the invasion will number 200 million, and by normal standards, they will occupy a territory a mile wide and eighty-seven miles long in their march south to Israel and Jerusalem to wage war against Israel and Jesus Christ at the Battle of Armageddon.

Unlike the first demons released from the abyss, these demons seemed to be mounted on some type of hellish horses whose heads look like lions; they had smoke, fire, and brimstone billowing out of their mouths. The riders wore fiery red breastplates. A similar description is given in the typology of the Babylonians' and Medes' battle against Nineveh in Nahum 2–3.

The source of this invasion is the Euphrates River, where sin and evil entered humanity (Zechariah 5:8–11; Genesis 3:1–8) in the garden of Eden. It is also where the false world religions began (Genesis 4:3, 10:9, 14) with Nimrod. This is also the place where it will all end (Revelation 17–18). We will study commercial and religious Babylon later in the book.

The damage described by this army will result in the deaths of a third of humanity, an additional **1 billion people.** Once again, we see the mercy and the intervention of God with the setting of limits on this invasion and war. God commanded the war would last for only thirteen months (v. 15), but it is recorded that people will not repent.

In verses 20 and 21, we read of people who were not killed but did not repent of the "works of their hands," including spiritual works; devil worship; worship of idols of gold, silver, brass, stone, wood, and dead gods. We can note the consistency of Scripture and God's Word from Belshazzar's feast in Daniel 5 and Ezekiel's vision in Ezekiel 8. People will worship the creature more than the Creator if they have rejected Jesus Christ (Romans 1:18–32).

Verse 21 tells us that these people did not repent of their physical sins, murders (John 8:44), or their sorceries (the Greek word here is *pharmakeion,* our word for pharmacy), drug crimes, fornication, sex crimes, and thefts. There is a rising crime epidemic in America today, and the newspapers offer stories of how most of today's violent crimes are tied to drugs or drug addiction.

PART VI

A LITTLE BOOK IS OPENED IN HEAVEN: REVELATION CHAPTER 10

1. The mighty angel and the "Little Book"—10:1–7
2. The end is near: "thou must prophesy"—10:8–11

In Revelation 9, we witnessed the opening of the fifth and sixth trumpet judgments, the demonic attack on humanity led by Satan, and the release of the four angels bound in the Euphrates. God in His mercy limited the afflictions on humanity to five months for the fifth trumpet judgment and thirteen months for the sixth trumpet judgment. God demonstrated His mercy also by keeping safe the 144,000 sealed Jewish male evangelists with the mark of the Living God on their foreheads.

For humanity's lack of repentance for its spiritual sins of worshipping the devil, for its sins of murder, theft, drugs, and sexual immorality, the judgment from the sixth trumpet resulted in the deaths of **1 billion at the hands of Satan's** demonic army. This demonic army rode into battle on hellish beasts that looked like horses, with heads like lions, with fire, smoke, and brimstone billowing out of their mouths, and they had tails like the heads of serpents that could bite.

Revelation 10 is another interlude or intermission chapter that once again affirmed Jesus' deity, authority, and mystery. In the theological and doctrinal context of chapter 10, we see another face of the will of God: "that His Word will be proclaimed throughout time to humanity by the prophets and the Word of God will not return void; but accomplish its purpose" (Amos 3:7; Isaiah 55:11). The Bible tells us, "Heaven and earth shall pass away but the Word of God will endure forever" (Mark 13:31). Revelation 10 is a relatively short chapter, but the correlation between the prophecy of this section of Scripture and the Old Testament prophecies are the link of Scripture comparison that binds the two testaments in one book.

"Forever O LORD, thy word is settled in heaven" (Psalm 119:89). "The counsel of the LORD, standeth forever to all generations" (Psalm 33:11).

In Revelation 10:1, John saw Jesus Christ clothed with a cloud (Revelation 1:7; Acts 1:9) and with a rainbow on His head (Revelation 4:3; Ezekiel 1:28). His face was as a sun (Revelation 1:16), and His feet were as pillars of fire (Revelation 1:15). From these reference verses, we know John the apostle was seeing Jesus Christ.

In verse 2, Jesus had a little book open. This little book is not the entire book that Christ had in Revelation 5:7. Please note the words in Matthew 1:1: "The Book of the generations of Jesus Christ." The Bible is Christocentric, and this is captured in the Old Testament, in Psalm 40:7: "Then said I, Lo, I come in the volume of the book, it is written about me." The little book of this passage contained only a portion of the Word of God, not the entire Bible. This little book contained the information Jesus Christ wanted John to know and to prophesy.

He set His right foot upon the sun, and His left foot on the earth. Psalm 95:5 and Haggai 2:6 read: "The sea is his and he made it, and his hands formed the dry land" and "I will shake the heavens and the earth, and the sea and the dry land."

In verse 3, He cried with a loud voice as when a lion roars (Revelation 5:5, the lion of the tribe of Judah), and when Christ cried, the seven thunders uttered their voices (Psalm 29:3–9), "and the voice of the Lord is upon the face of the waters, the glory of God thundereth, the Lord is upon many waters."

In verse 4, we read, "and when the seven thunders had uttered their voices, I was about to write [Revelation 1:11]: and I heard a voice from heaven saying unto me, seal up those things which the seven thunders uttered and write them not" (Daniel 8:26, 12:4, 9; 2 Corinthians 12:4). There are some areas of the Word that God gave to certain prophets and apostles for their eyes and ears only. The seven thunders is such a case. John heard them but could not record them just as God had instructed Daniel and Paul not to write.

Why could John not write these utterances? The message was for the Jewish nation at the end time. Here are some possible answers to this question, but they are not grounded in Scripture. The voice of the thunders might be revealed to the Jewish nation in the tribulation by the two witnesses in Revelation 11 or possibly by the 144,000 Jewish male virgin evangelists with the seal of the Living God. Remember that after Revelation 4:1 with the rapture of the church, God was dealing with Israel, not the church, which was in heaven at that point.

What did the thunders say? We don't know and possibly will never know. This is very much like the conversation Peter had with Jesus on the shore of Galilee about John's purpose in the ministry. Christ rebuked Peter: "What is that to thee?" Many believe that one day we will know everything, but Scripture does not support that belief. We will never be omniscient, we will never know everything about God (Isaiah 55:8–9), and Scripture is silent in certain areas; the Bible does not record how much time elapsed between Genesis 1:1 and 1:3, nor does it say how long Adam and Eve were in the garden before they sinned.

In verses 5 and 6, John saw Jesus standing on the sea and earth with His hands lifted to heaven, and swore by Him who lived forever (Deuteronomy 33:27, the eternal God is thy refuge). Jesus Christ said that God His Father created heaven, earth, and the sea and all the things in them (Genesis 1:1; Revelation 4:11). He also said that there would be time no longer; this means no more delays as time would not stop until the new heaven and the new earth were revealed and presented in eternity future (Revelation 21–22).

In verse 7, we read, "But in the days of the voice of the seventh angel when he shall begin to sound" (Revelation 11:15). This, however, does not give us a clue about the voice of the thunders.

We are told that He sounded out the mystery of God (Matthew 13:11); these were His parables and prophecies. In Matthew 25:14–19, we read the parable about the master who was away for a long time. It has now been almost 2,000 years since Jesus Christ ascended to heaven (Acts 1:8–11), and His promised return is fast approaching (John 14:6; Matthew 24, 32–35) for our **terminal generation.**

The passage "Should be finished, as he hath declared to his servants the prophets" is from Amos 3:7 in the Old Testament.

There is a break between verses 1 through 7 and verses 8 through 11. In the former verses, the deity of Jesus Christ was reaffirmed, and in verses 8 through 11, God's grace, mercy, and love and His charge to share the Word was given to John and everyone.

"And the voice which I heard from heaven [Revelation 4:1] spake to unto me again and said, God and take the little book which is open." Revelation is not a closed book; it is available to all to read, to hear, and to understand the blessings and the warnings. The book is in the hand of the angel, Christ, who is standing upon the sea and the earth.

"And I went up to the angel, and said unto him, Give me the little book. And he said unto me, Take it [Ezekiel 2:8–9, 3:1–3] and eat it up." Why are we to consume God's Word?

1. To be approved of God (2 Timothy 2:15)
2. To be saved by God through Jesus Christ, the Living Word (John 1:1, 2; Timothy 3:14–15)
3. To be kept from sin (Psalm 119:11)
4. To walk in the light of righteousness (Psalm 119:105)
5. The Word of God is the Bread of Life and the Living Water that sustains us from day to day (John 6:33–35)

John was told that the book would make his belly bitter (Jeremiah 20:14–18) because the Word of God revealed to all humanity by the illumination of the Holy Ghost would convict humanity of its sins, transgressions, and iniquities before the Lord and assure people of the consequences of their sins (Romans 6:23; James 1:15; Romans 5:12). According to the text, the Word of God was sweet like honey (Psalm 19:10), and in the Word, we find comfort from or sorrows, confidence in our weakness, healing in our sickness, and forgiveness from our sins.

In verse 10, John ate the book; it was sweet to the taste but became bitter.

In verse 11, Jesus Christ commanded John to prophesy (Jeremiah 25:15–16; Isaiah 6:1–8) before many people, nations, tongues, and kings. The command to prophesy again is a dual-reference command in prophecy.

John's writing of the Word of Christ is as compelling, convicting, and convincing today for our **terminal generation** as it was twenty centuries ago. John's prophetic words confirm that God's Word and salvation are for all people regardless of race, color, creed, or stature (Acts 10:34).

This chapter closes with the command that the Word of God was to be proclaimed, preached, witnessed, taught, and shared (2 Corinthians 5:17–20; Acts 1:8, 5:42; Matthew 28:19).

The Times of the Gentiles: Chapter 11

1. The tribulation temple in Jerusalem—11:1–2
2. The two witnesses in Jerusalem—11:3–12
3. The second woe judgment—11:13–14
4. The trumpet judgments resumed, and the seventh trumpet sounds—11:15–19

Revelation 10 is the second interlude chapter in which Christ's deity was revealed, the voice of the seven thunders was sealed until the end of days, and Old Testament prophecy was compared to New Testament prophecy. God's enduring love for humanity was recorded in the words of Christ to John, who was to consume and share the Word of God from the little book with all humanity.

In verses 1 and 2, John received Christ's command to measure the tribulation temple in Jerusalem. We do not want to get lost here in Revelation 11, but the temple was going to be rebuilt in Jerusalem following the peace treaty brokered by the anti-Christ with Israel. Currently, a Muslim mosque sits on the temple mount, but the plans and materials for the rebuilding of the temple are in place today, in 2014. There are several excellent websites on the rebuilding of the temple and the progress of the word in Israel today. Animal sacrifices will resume during the tribulation era, and at the midpoint of the seven years of the tribulation, the temple will be desecrated by the anti-Christ and the false prophet. This was covered in Daniel 9:27 and in Jesus' Olivet Discourse on the last days in Matthew 24:15. This event will be covered in greater detail in Revelation 13:1–18, when Satan's image and idol were placed in the rebuilt temple as shown by the typology of the desecration of the temple in Jerusalem by Antiochus Epiphanes. He was the prototype of the man of sin, the anti-Christ who sacrificed a sow upon the altar of the temple in Jerusalem and entered the Holy of Holies (Daniel 11:31).

The phrase *abomination of desolation* occurs three times in Daniel 9:27 and 12:11 in reference to the *beast or the man of sin* in 2 Thessalonians 2:3–4. It is identified with Matthew 24:15.

John received a reed, which translates as a nine-foot ruler (Ezekiel 40:5; Zechariah 2:1–2) and was told to measure the tribulation temple and record the identity of the worshippers. God is always interested in those who worship Him.

The outer court was to be left out; it was known as the court of the Gentiles, for it was given to the Gentiles, and Jerusalem was not to be tread under the foot of the Gentiles for forty-two months, 1,260 days, or three and a half years of the tribulation era according to Christ (Luke 21:24; Daniel 7:25, 12:7; Revelation 12:6, 14, 13:5).

Verses 3 through 5 reveal the two witnesses who stood before God; these verses raise heavily debated questions as to their identities. The Bible is clear in their description, their length and location of ministry, their audience, their authority, and their death and resurrection following forty-two months of ministry at the Western Wall in Jerusalem. Some hold that these two witnesses before God were Elijah and Enoch and use Hebrews 9:27 as support for their view. Hebrews 9:27 tells us that all were appointed to die, and since these two did not experience physical death, they would be sent back to stand as the two witnesses of Revelation 11 before God.

Genesis 5:22 and 2 Kings 2:1–12 deal with Elijah and the rapture of Enoch. The witnesses would die martyrs' deaths following their forty-two months of ministry. Enoch, however, does not seem to fit the profile of a prophet as he did not have the qualifications for being one of the two witnesses to the Jewish nation in this passage for several reasons.

1. Although Enoch was a righteous man, he was a Gentile.
2. Enoch never performed signs, wonders, and miracles and never prophesied.
3. Enoch serves as a much better example in the Old Testament as a typology of the rapture of the New Testament church. God took him before the flood; likewise, God will take the New Testament church out of the world before the tribulation judgments.

Some hold these two witnesses were Elijah and Moses and reference Malachi 4:5–6, which foretells that God will send Elijah during the tribulation before the great and terrible day of the Lord. Matthew 17:3 states that Elijah and Moses appeared with God and before Jesus Christ on the Mount of Transfiguration Matthew 17:3. Support for this view is found in the fact that Elijah withheld rain on Israel for three years, and this will be repeated in the tribulation era (1 Kings 17:1; Revelation 11:6).

Text that supports the view that Moses was one of the two witnesses range from Jude 9 in the New Testament, where we learn Moses did not die a natural death, and Satan attempted to steal his body so God would not be able to use him against the anti-Christ during the tribulation. Additionally, we read in Exodus 7:19 and Revelation 11:6 that Moses turned water into blood.

Israel reveres Elijah and Moses as their greatest prophets; the whole world will be stirred by their preaching and prophecy during the tribulation era as they perform signs, wonders, and miracles authenticating their Master and His message.

These two witnesses are to proclaim the Word of God to the Jewish nation in sackcloth (burlap) robes and stand before all humanity as God's two olive trees that will identify them as Jewish prophets and to stand as God's anointed Lamb stands (Zechariah 4:1–14). Prophets and pastors declare that the Light of the World is Jesus Christ, the Living Word of God, the promises of God that all people must be born again! Sackcloth is a sign of mourning, and the word is used forty-six times in the Bible. Job in his suffering wore sackcloth, Jacob wore sackcloth as he mourned Joseph,

Samuel wore sackcloth as he mourned Israel's King, and the Gentile king of Nineveh wore sackcloth and mourned for his nation's and his own sins.

God will empower these two witnesses to destroy their enemies during their forty-two months of ministry just as their enemies will attempt to destroy them. We must remember when serving and following God's perfect will for our lives that we also are indestructible until the ministry is completed. These two witnesses have God's authority to destroy their enemies with fire from their mouths, to prevent rain for three and a half years in Israel, to turn water to blood, and to smite the earth with every kind of plague. In Exodus 7:14 and 12:36, Egypt suffered ten plagues, and God brought the Israelites out of Egypt.

Take particular notice of Revelation 11:6: "as often as they will." This is the level of trust God has for these two witnesses. We should ask not how much God trusts us but how much we trust God. Will we trust Him with our eternal souls? Will we trust the truth of His Word concerning the **terminal generation?** Will we trust Him to save and keep us from the hour of tribulation? In Hebrews 11:1, God took away our fears and misunderstandings about t*rust and faith:* "Now faith is the substance of things hoped for, the evidence of things not seen."

In verses 7 through 12, when the two witnesses had finished their testimony, the anti-Christ was allowed to kill them. Let us look at the testimony of the witnesses. God never developed a plan B for salvation; God's Word is consistent, self-authenticating, and without confusion. God never changed His plan, method, or means of salvation, and just as the apostle Paul was sent with God's message for the Gentile nations in the church age, God turned His attention to Israel, and the message is the same.

Seven great Bible truths are captured in the testimony of a saint.

1. All people have an inborn knowledge of God (Romans 1:18).
2. All people reject God (Romans 1:21).
3. All people are guilty before God (Romans 1:32).
4. 4.   All people are condemned for rejecting God (Romans 1:28).

5. God has only one plan of salvation (Romans 5:9–10; John 3:16, 36; Romans 10:13).
6. People cannot come to God apart from faith in Jesus Christ (Romans 3:21–26; John 14:6).
7. Christ commanded the church to make the gospel known to all people (Matthew 28:18–20; Acts 1:8; 2 Corinthians 5:17–20).

The word *beast* in verse 11 is the first of thirty-five uses of this word in Revelation. In this passage, we see the limited authority God allowed Satan. Satan and his anti-Christ could not touch the two witnesses or a humble servant of Christ without the Lord's permission (Job 1:12, 2:6).

The Bible offers the testimony of many martyred and faithful servants who finished their ministry and testimony before their deaths. Stephen in Acts 7 is a great example of a faithful servant, as is Paul, as we read in his epistles. In Revelation 12:11, the Bible instructs us in the power of our personal testimony, the power of the Word of God, and the blood of the Lamb: "They overcame Satan, by the blood of the Lamb, and the word of their testimony, and they loved not their own lives unto death."

To show his contempt for God's chosen witnesses, Satan did not allow their bodies to be buried but left them for the world to view and to rot in the streets of Jerusalem. We know the city by this passage: "in that great city which spiritually is called Sodom [because of immorality] and Egypt [because of its worldliness] where our Lord was crucified." Jesus Christ was crucified outside Jerusalem, not Babylon or Rome. This is an important clue as to the location of religious Babylon when we get to Revelation 17–18 in this book.

All the earth saw the death of the two witnesses in Jerusalem and celebrated their deaths by giving and receiving gifts—a hellish Christmas holiday. In Revelation 11:10, the word *rejoice* is used, but it is the only time it is used in Revelation. Sad and lost men and women rejoice and take pleasure in sin, the suffering of the saints, and the slander of God's Word (Romans 1:18–32).

After three and a half days, God's Spirit (Genesis 2:7) entered the two witnesses who were killed and left to rot; they stood, and a ***great fear fell upon the masses that viewed their death and then their resurrection!***

In verses 11 through 14, we read of three "greats": a great fear, a great voice, and a great earthquake. Great fear came about because the world witnessed the resurrection of the two dead witnesses; their cadaverous hue changed to a rosy glow, and their stiff limbs moved (Ezekiel 37, valley of dry bones vision). The two stood before the Lord. The crowd moved back and then moved in for a closer look. The smell of death was no longer in the air; they saw the glorious sight of the dead raised to life. A great voice was heard when Christ commanded, "Come up here." The two witnesses were taken up to heaven in a cloud as their enemies watched.

A great earthquake will level a tenth of Jerusalem and kill 7,000, including prominent people, as death is no respecter of persons. But the faithful remnant of Jews will be afraid and praise and give glory to God. The Jews praying at the Wailing Wall today pray for their Messiah to return and to restore them. That won't be much longer; Jesus will answer their prayers of the last twenty-one centuries. This ends the second woe of the trumpet judgments.

In verses 15 through 18, the seventh angel sounded his trumpet to announce Christ's Second Advent, which occurred in Revelation 19. Revelation is not in chronological order; this portion of chapter 11 is parenthetical to Revelation 19; it is a foretelling of the Second Advent.

The angel delivered the glorious news that Jesus Christ was conquering and taking the world's kingdoms for His own and would rule nations in a theocracy. Those in heaven rejoiced, but the nations of the world were angry. This angel prepared us for what is ahead in history.

The Mysteries of God

The mystery of God, His parables, and His prophecy were explained in chapter 10, but now it is necessary to expand this definition. Verses 1 through 10 in 2 Peter 3 capture the mind, heart, and state of humanity in our terminal generation. People no longer look, long for, or believe in the promised return of Jesus Christ. Many have asked, "If there is a loving God, why does He allow so much pain and suffering? Why are there wars, diseases, starvation, and abuse? Why are there deadly natural disasters?" Although heartrending, such questions reveal a lack of understanding of humanity's sorry state. God created a perfect world with ample food and peace; it was through Satan and Adam and Eve's fall that the world and humanity were corrupted.

We live in a fallen, sin-sick world, and because we are separated from Jesus Christ, we will accomplish only evil. Matters will get progressively worse as humanity indulges more and more in sin. The grace of God was revealed when He sent His Son as the sacrifice for sin and provided salvation for all who believed and accepted Him. In 2 Peter 3:1–10, specifically verses 8 and 9, we learn the reason for God's delay in judgment upon sin and the establishment of Christ's theocratic rule as given in Isaiah 9:6–7. In Peter's address to the skeptic in 2 Peter 3, we find the answer in verses 8–9.

> But beloved by not ignorant of this one thing, that one day with the Lord is as a thousand years, and a thousand years as one day. The Lord is not slack concerning his promise as some men count slackness, but is longsuffering to usward, not willing any should perish, but that all should come to repentance.

God is never bound by time, only by His promises.

In verse 19, the temple of God in heaven and the Ark of the Covenant was there as seen and recorded in Isaiah 6:1–8. Exodus 25:9, 20; Hebrews 8:2, 5, 9:24; and Revelation 14–15:5, 6:8, 16:1, and 17 also refer to the temple of God in heaven and the Ark of the Covenant.

John saw the Ark of the Covenant or the Testament that held the Ten Commandments God wrote for Moses on stone tablets for the children of Israel. John saw and heard the lightning, voices, thundering, the earthquake, and great hail. All of these were prophetic of the vial or bowl judgments in the coming chapters.

Part VII

The Seven Personages: Revelation Chapters 12–13

1. The woman Israel—12:1–2
2. The red dragon Satan—12:3–4
3. The Christ child—12:5–6
4. The Archangel Michael—12:7–12
5. Satan and Israel in the tribulation—12:13–16
6. The Jewish remnant—12:17
7. The beast of the sea, the anti-Christ—13:1–10
8. The beast of the earth, the false prophet and his mark, 666—13:11–18

In Revelation 11, we read of the apostle John's measuring the tribulation temple in Jerusalem and taking note of the faithful remnant worshipping God. We were introduced to the two witnesses that stood before God and prophesied for three and a half years at the Wailing Wall; we learned of the trust the Lord placed in them, their protection, and finally their death at the hands of the anti-Christ. Three days later, they were miraculously resurrected and ascended into heaven at the summons of the Lord. Chapter 11 ended with the completion of the second and third woe and the temple of God in heaven being opened.

In Revelation 12, we need to remember God was dealing with Israel. The church comprising all born-again believers in Christ was caught away in the rapture in Revelation 4:1, and Jesus Christ introduced the first five personages in Revelation 12 to us through John's words.

In verses 1 and 2, John saw a great wonder or sign in heaven, a woman clothed with the sun, and the moon was under her feet. These first two verses set the context and the scene of this passage as being Israel, the twelve tribes of Jacob, and the suffering Jewish nation waiting for deliverance.

Genesis 37:7–11 tells the story of Joseph's dream that his brothers, father, and mother would bow down to him. This was fulfilled in Egypt when God raised Joseph to a position of power and authority under Pharaoh. Joseph in Scripture serves as a typology of Jesus Christ. Joseph was sold into slavery, unjustly tried and imprisoned, but was exalted and served as the redeemer of the nation (Exodus 1:1–5).

The **crown of the twelve stars represents the twelve sons of Jacob.** It is important to reference Genesis 32:27–28, when God changed Jacob's name from "Deceiver" to "Israel," power with God. Each of the stars represents one of the twelve tribes of Israel.

In verse 2, we read, "And she being with child cried, travailing in birth, and pained to be delivered." We must look at Israel historically and symbolically in this passage as a woman who was pregnant and in hard labor since Genesis. Following Adam and Eve's sin, God pronounced judgment upon the serpent, the woman, and Adam and gave the first messianic prophecy in the Bible to send His Redeemer, Jesus Christ (Genesis 3:15).

The delivery of the Redeemer as promised by the Father was repeated throughout Scripture to the patriarch Abram in Genesis 12:3, to Moses in Exodus 12:11–13, to Isaiah in Isaiah 7:14 and 9:6–7, and to the minor prophet Micah in Micah 5:2. The pain to be delivered was fulfilled in the birth of the Messiah in Matthew 1:18–25 and Luke 1 and 2, which Israel sadly refused by rejecting and crucifying Jesus Christ (Luke 19:41–44, 23:20–21, 27:25; John 19:14–15).

In verses 3 through 6, John saw another wonder in heaven, **a great red dragon with** seven heads and crowns and ten horns. There is no question that this vicious creature is Satan, who was given at least seven titles in Revelation 12 alone.

From Daniel's prophecy in Daniel 7 through 9, we learn that the beast and the horn visions represent world empires. The last world empire is the revived Roman Empire from Nebuchadnezzar's vision of the giant statue; the head of gold is the **Babylonian Empire;** the chest of silver is the **Mede and Persian Empire;** the belly of brass/bronze is the **Greek Empire** of Alexander the Great; the legs of iron is the **Roman Empire;** and finally, the feet of iron mingled with clay is the **revived Roman Empire** of the last days and tribulation times for the **terminal generation.** It is out of this final world empire that the anti-Christ will be revealed and become the political, military, economic, and religious ruler of the world in the last days until defeated by Jesus Christ in the Battle of Armageddon.

The **great red dragon** was great because of its vast power possessed by Satan (Matthew 4:8–9). It was red because it was the first murderer (John 8:44). It was a dragon because it was vicious (2 Corinthians 6:15). It was an **old serpent** because it was in the garden of Eden (Genesis 3:3). A serpent reminds us of the form Satan took to tempt Eve (Genesis 3:1–8). It was the **devil,** one who slandered God (Revelation 12:10; Job 1:9–11; Zechariah 3:1–7; Luke 22:31). **Satan was** the adversary (1 Peter 5:8) and **the deceiver of the world. Note that** the devil deceived not only people but also angels. His tail drew the third part of the angelic host away with him when he rebelled against God (Isaiah 14:12–17). These verse translated means that Satan literally dragged them down with him. Acts 14:19 and Ezekiel 28:11–19 amplify this passage.

The beast was the persecutor of the woman, who was Israel, and the Christ child. Throughout Bible history, Satan persecuted Israel and attempted to destroy the good seed of God. **The beast was a hater of Christ because Christ was incarnated, resurrected, and ascended into heaven**, where He reigns (Psalm 2:6–9).

Notice that in verse 4, Satan was waiting to devour the child as soon as He was born. Herod the Great attempted to kill the Christ child when Jesus was born (Matthew 2:13). Notice that in verse 5, the child is Christ (Matthew 1:21), who will rule all nations (Isaiah 9:6–7) and was caught up to God and His throne in heaven (Acts 1:11).

In verse 6, we see the woman flee to a place prepared by God in the wilderness. In the wilderness during the last days of the tribulation, God will provide a refuge for the faithful, believing remnant who worship the one, true Living God. The location of the refuge of God in the wilderness has often been thought to be **Petra, which was** referred to as the rainbow city and once had 275,000 inhabitants. The city is accessible only through a narrow canyon wide enough for only two horses abreast. The cliffs surrounding Petra are 700 feet high, and the buildings and rooms are cut out of stone. There are fresh water springs, and wild fig trees grow there sheltered from the desert heat. God will once again provide, protect, and shelter His chosen people during the darkest days of **Jacob's troubles.**

In verses 7 through 12, John saw a **great war in heaven. Note** that this was in the latter days of the second half of the great tribulation and in the final three and a half years of the anti-Christ's reign. Michael the Archangel and his angels fought against Satan, the dragon, and Satan was cast out of heaven.

Satan will experience five falls from heaven. The first was after he rebelled against God (Ezekiel 28:11–19). Jesus Christ testified as being present during this first fall of Satan, and Jesus warned His seventy disciples not to rejoice that the evil spirits were subject to them in Jesus' name but to rejoice because their names were written in the Book of Life. Jesus said that He had seen Satan fall like lightning to earth (Luke 10:17–20). Satan will fall four additional times, first to Michael, again when bound in the abyss for 1,000 years, and again when defeated during the **Battle of Armageddon and the Final Battle of Armageddon,** and last, when he is cast into hell for eternity.

Significantly, Satan currently has access to heaven and stands before the throne of God, accusing believers night and day. But for the grace of God, we have an advocate with the Father, Jesus Christ, who intercedes for us before the throne of God night and day in this present age of grace, the church age. John heard a voice say, "Satan is cast to earth and no longer accuses the saints before the Throne of God."

In verses 10 and 11, we read of the **four blood-bought freedoms** we have in Jesus Christ.

1. **Salvation** (John 3:16; Romans 10:9–10), forgiveness of sin (1 John 1:9), freedom from the wrath of God (Romans 5:1), and freedom from condemnation (Romans 8:1).
2. **Power** for abundant life to minister and bear fruit (Philippians 4:13).
3. **A share in the kingdom of God and Christ** (Matthew 5:3–12; Galatians 4:4–7).
4. **The promises of Christ** that we shall overcome Satan (1 Corinthians 10:13).

There is rejoicing in heaven, but woe to the earth, for the devil has come down and knows his time is short (verse 12), and his great wrath is focused on Israel and Christ.

In verses 13 through 16, Satan's persecution of Israel during the great tribulation is reflected in the Jewish people's suffering of affliction and persecution throughout the ages; it serves as a graphic warning to all who reject Jesus Christ. When Jesus Christ was tried before the Sanhedrin, in the course of Christ seven illegal and biased trials Jesus was delivered to Pilate and accused of blasphemy. Pilate told the Jews he could find no fault in Jesus, but the people cried out that He should be crucified (Matthew 27:22–25). Pilate washed his hands, saying that he was innocent of the blood of an innocent man. The mob cried out to Pilate, "Let his blood be upon us and our children." Hence, the blood of Christ has been upon the Jews for the past 2,000 years. Anti-Semitism has been inflicted upon the Jewish nation since that terrible declaration before Pontius Pilate at the judgment seat in Jerusalem.

Satan has attempted to exterminate the Jewish nation by *enslaving* (Exodus 2), *drowning* (Exodus 14), *starving* (Exodus 16), *tempting* (Numbers 14), *cursing* (Numbers 23), *capturing* (2 Kings 17, 24), *swallowing* (Jonah 2), *burning* (Daniel 3), *devouring* (Daniel 6), and *hanging* (Esther 3). We can add to this list the 7 million Jews exterminated by the Nazis. The Jews were hunted down, imprisoned, forced into slave labor, starved to death, executed in gas chambers, burned in the furnaces, and murdered by every cruel means imaginable and discarded into unmarked graves. But through it all, the mercy of God prevailed, and a remnant is preserved to this day.

Israel will be empowered by God and symbolically mount up on wings of eagles and will flee to a place prepared by God, possibly Petra as stated earlier, and the nourishment and provision will last for three and a half years. Note Daniel 9:27, 11:31, and 12:11 in comparison with the Olivet Discourse in Matthew 24:15–22. It is a small thing for God to protect and provide for the remnant for three and a half years; He fed 1.5 million of His children in the wilderness for forty years! In that day, Israel will flee in haste just as it did from Egypt.

Satan, the serpent, will attempt to destroy Israel as its people flee with a counterfeit miracle, a flood of water to swallow them up, similar to the flood of Noah's day. **God, however,** will open the mouth of the earth and swallow all the water sent by Satan. This is not the first time God stopped the waters. He parted the Red Sea for Israel and He stopped the waters of the Jordan River while they were raging so Joshua could lead the Israelites across. God has opened the earth's mouth before in judgment; God judged Korah, and the earth opened and took him and his followers. God will prevail again over evil (2 Chronicles 20:23–24).

In verse 17, the Jewish remnant became the focus of Satan's attention. To a lesser degree, this is seen historically and prophetically in the destruction of Jerusalem by Titus in AD 70 and the dispersion of the Jews, fulfilling the prophecy of Jesus Christ when Israel rejected the Messiah. This persecution was seen in the ten periods of the historic persecution of the Jews and Christians by the Roman Empire as recorded in John's letters to the seven churches in Revelation 2 and 3. In the great tribulation, the revived Roman Empire will again come against God's chosen people. At this point of the tribulation, the persecution of Israel by the anti-Christ and the nations of the world are for four reasons.

1. They will come to capture Israel's wealth and resources.
2. They will want Israel's strategic location in the Middle East from which to command and control the world's economy and religious worship.
3. Because the remnant of Israel in the tribulation keeps the Commandments of God.
4. Because Israel in the tribulation will profess that Jesus Christ is its Messiah and Savior.

The Seven Personages Continued: Revelation 13

1. The beast of the sea, the anti-Christ—13:1–10
2. The beast of the earth, the false prophet and his mark, 666—Revelation 13:11–18

We closed chapter 12 having observed the first five of the seven personages: the woman, who was Israel; the dragon, who was Satan; the Child, who was Jesus; the archangel, who was Michael, and the Jewish remnant, who were faithful to God during the great tribulation, kept the Commandments, and embraced Jesus Christ as their Messiah.

In Revelation 13, the sixth and seventh personages are revealed: the beast of the sea, who was the anti-Christ, and the beast of the earth, who was the false prophet. These two complete the unholy trinity that opposed God, Jesus Christ, the Holy Spirit, the saints, and Jerusalem and deceived the nations. Satan was the power possessing and directing the actions of the anti-Christ and the false prophet.

In verse 1, when John saw a beast rise up out of the sea, this was symbolic as described in the Bible as rising out of the sea of humanity and the Gentile nations. From earlier chapters, we know this beast is a man who will come to power following the rapture of the church; his rise to power will be out of the European Union and through diplomacy, he will subdue three of the European nations and rule over the remaining ten nations. Symbolically, this man, the anti-Christ of the latter days, John saw as having seven heads and ten horns, and upon his horns were ten crowns or diadems, speaking of an earthly rule, and upon his head was the name "Blasphemy."

This passage from Revelation 13 relates to the prophet Daniel's vision in Daniel 7:24 and forward to Revelation 17:12; it is translated as ten kings, and the entire vision is the last form of Gentile world power, a confederated, ten-kingdom empire covering the revived Roman Empire. Its new emperor will be the beast of the sea, the anti-Christ of 2 Thessalonians 2:1–12.

What are the beast's characteristics?

1. He will be an intellectual genius (Daniel 8:23).
2. He will be an oratorical genius (Daniel 11:36).
3. He will be a political genius (Revelation 17:11–12).
4. He will be a commercial genius (Revelation 13:16–17).
5. He will be a military genius (Revelation 6:2, 13:2).
6. He will be a religious genius (Revelation 13:8; 2 Thessalonians 2:4).

The beast will speak great words against the Most High and will wear out the saints of the Most High (Daniel 7:25). The kings will do according to his will, and he will exalt himself above every god and speak blasphemy against God. This is consistent with the character and nature of Satan as described in Isaiah 14:12–17 and Daniel 11:36. The beast is called

1. the man of sin (2 Thessalonians 2:3),
2. the son of perdition (2 Thessalonians 2:8),
3. the wicked one (2 Thessalonians 2:8),
4. the willful king (Daniel 11:36),
5. the beast (Revelation 11:7), and
6. the little horn (from Daniel 7:8).

There are three schools of thought on the personage of the beast of the sea, the anti-Christ.

1. This personage is symbolic only of the depravity of society at the time and does not represent a king or global ruler; it reflects humanity's nature in general during the time of global political and economic turmoil. This position, however, is inconsistent with the context and content of the Bible.
2. This personage will be a resurrected individual based on Revelation 13:3 and 17:8, but this does not fit the interpretation of the Scriptures according to proper Bible exegesis. The person identified by this particular school of thought is Judas Iscariot, who Christ identified as the son of perdition. This particular phrase is found twice in the New Testament, when Christ called Judas by that name and when Paul the apostle spoke of the anti-Christ. Although Judas Iscariot betrayed Jesus Christ with a kiss for thirty pieces of silver, he committed suicide. There is no biblical basis or scriptural text in support of the resurrection of Judas, who was condemned and is suffering in Hades for rejecting Christ. Judas Iscariot and Antiochus Epiphanes are parallel typologies of the anti-Christ of the last days of our terminal generation.
3. The beast of the sea, according to Scripture, will be a Gentile who comes to power following the rapture of the church, rising out of

the European League of Nations. The anti-Christ is a literal person possessed, controlled, and motivated by his master, Satan.

In verse 2, the beast John saw was like a leopard with feet like a bear's and a mouth like a lion's. The dragon, Satan, gave him his power, seat, and authority. The three animals mentioned here are from Daniel's prophetic vision in Daniel 7:4–6 and serve as symbols of the empires that preceded Rome and yet whose qualities were carried into the Roman Empire. The empire of the leopard represented the Macedonian or Greek Empire for its swiftness of conquest. By age twenty-nine, Alexander the Great had conquered the known world. The empire of the bear represented the Persian Empire for its tenacity of purpose. The empire of the lion represented the Babylonian Empire for it voracity.

The anti-Christ's rise to power will be fulfilled by

1. Satan (Revelation 13:2; 2 Thessalonians 2:3, 9–12).
2. Through the permission of the Holy Spirit. The presentation and the appearing of the anti-Christ will be hindered and prevented by the Holy Spirit until the rapture of the church (2 Thessalonians 2:2–3).
3. Through the formation of a ten-nation organization in Europe. These ten nations or ten horns are the dictators from the European League of Nations in Daniel 7:7. The majority of this prophecy remains to be fulfilled in the very near future following the rapture.
4. Through the cooperation with the world's false religious systems and the ecumenical movement today that attempts to bring all world religions together. Despite some religious similarities among the major world religions, there is a major point of theological and doctrinal separation between Christianity and all others. In Christ Jesus alone do we have access to the grace of God for the assurance of salvation by faith alone, not by works, ceremony, traditions, or personal merit.
5. Through his charisma and ability to sway the masses.
6. Through a counterfeit resurrection. At the midpoint of his rule, the anti-Christ will be attacked; this will possibly be an attempted

assassination. He will receive severe wounds to his arm and eye (Zechariah 11:17). It is noteworthy that a number of world rulers, including Napoleon and Hitler, sustained wounds to their arms and eyes.

7. Through a false peace treaty with Israel and the world that he will violate at the midpoint of the tribulation period and usher in the final 1,260 days of the great tribulation.

The three reasons for the world to accept the anti-Christ as its Messiah are the universal ignorance of the prophetic words of God (Matthew 22:29), an outpouring of fierce demonic activity in the last days leading up to the rapture of the church (1 Timothy 4:1; 2 Timothy 3:1–7), and humanity's many empty and hungry souls (Luke 11:24–26).

Verses 3 through 10 deal with the activities of the anti-Christ during his seven-year reign. He will begin by controlling the Western European nations and gain political, economic, and military control initially. The United States is not mentioned in the end-time prophecy; there is only one vague reference in Scripture to America as being possibly one of England's lion cubs (Ezekiel 38:13). But it is vitally important to know that the fall of America in our *terminal generation* may happen early in 2015, and it will not be the result of a foreign invasion. America will cease to be a leading world power when its **national debt is so high that it cannot pay the interest on it.** In very late 2014 or early 2015, a swift change will occur in the global economy, and the dollar will no longer be the world's trade standard. I believe these events were set in motion when the United States got off the gold standard, initiated Social Security, established the Federal Reserve, loosened banking regulation for interstate banking, and departed from the Word of God.

There have been many financial tremors as the result of these changes. Consider the banking collapse due to subprime mortgage lending practices, banks' insufficient equity-to-debt ratios, the collapse of Wall Street, the auto industry bailout by the government, the recent government shutdowns, and the **Universal Health Care Act.** There is a looming **economic earthquake on the horizon** that will shake the very foundations of America, and this country's fall will be the result of unfettered greed, materialism, immorality, and the rejection of God's laws governing nations.

God judges all sin, the personal sins of humanity and the sins of a nation, including abortion on demand, same-sex marriages and civil unions, the legalization of drugs, gambling, prostitution, pornography, idolatry, and spiritual adultery. Jesus Christ said in John 16:33, "These things have I spoken unto you, that in me ye might have peace. In the world ye shall have tribulation: but be of good cheer; for I have overcome the world."

The Word of God reveals that the church will be taken away prior to the tribulation, but Christ told us there would also be times of trials for the saints prior to the rapture and the revealing of the anti-Christ. What possible signs and events can we expect to see in the coming year in America?

1. Frequent partial government shut-downs
2. Increased stock market manipulation by the federal reserve regarding prime interest rates for loans
3. Increased personal paperless financial transactions and an increase in personal unsecured credit card debt by the American public
4. The taxation of previously 501c3 tax-exempt organizations
5. An ever-increasing loss of personal privacy and national liberty
6. The expansion of Homeland Security forces and martial law
7. Increased use of presidential executive power to override Congress

The anti-Christ will have the amazing ability to *imitate Jesus Christ* and deceive the world into thinking he is the Messiah. Jesus Christ came in the image of the Father, but the anti-Christ will come in the image of Satan. He will be the second person of this hellish trinity, the anti-Christ empowered by Satan, who will come from the abyss, while Jesus Christ will come from heaven. The anti-Christ will be a savage beast, while Jesus Christ is the sacrificial Lamb of God. The anti-Christ will receive his power from Satan, but Jesus Christ receives His power from God. The anti-Christ will experience a counterfeit resurrection, but Jesus Christ experienced a true resurrection. The anti-Christ will receive worship from all unbelievers, but Jesus Christ is worshipped by the saints.

The greatest part of the anti-Christ's speeches and activity will occur during the last three and a half years of his reign, while Jesus Christ's earthly ministry lasted three and a half years, from His baptism to His ascension. The anti-Christ will attempt unsuccessfully to unite the offices of prophet, priest, and king, but in the last days, Jesus Christ will unite His offices at His Second Advent. The anti-Christ will kill his harlot wife, the apostate church, but Jesus Christ will glorify His holy bride, the sanctified church.

Verse 6 contains some closing thoughts in this chapter about all who dwell upon the earth worshipping him. Satan would have us believe that all people will worship him; it is Satan's sin and greatest desire to be like God and receive worship (Isaiah 14:12–13). But upon closer examination, the Word of God tells us, "Those written in the Lamb's Book of Life will not worship Satan." Here are some great questions for personal contemplation: Is your name written in the Lamb's Book of Life? Is your name written in heaven? Have you accepted Jesus Christ as your personal Savior, or will you choose to worship Satan?

Verse 9 is short, but it carries us back to the letters to the seven churches in Revelation 2 and 3: "If you have an ear, hear what God is saying to you today."

We must beware of false prophets; Satan has always had somebody ready to take the role of the anti-Christ in every generation for the past twenty-one centuries in his efforts to deceive humanity. Jesus Christ in the Olivet Discourse warned that in the last days there would be many who would claim to be the Messiah, the Christ, but be not deceived.

In July 1964, the *Reader's Digest* ran a condensed version of *A Gift of Prophecy* by Jeane Dixon, a false prophetess. The book concluded with this statement: "A child born in the Middle East on February 5, 1962 will revolutionize the world and eventually untie all the warring creeds, and sects into one all-embracing faith." The person who was the subject of Dixon's strongest and clearest visions was born a humble peasant, and humanity, according to Dixon, will begin to feel this man's force about 1980, and his power will grow mightily until 1999, at which time there will be peace on earth to all people of good will.

In 1 John 4:1–4, Jesus warned of false prophets in the last days and of the anti-Christ in the last days. Jesus told the Pharisees, "I am come in my Father's name and ye receive me not; if another shall come in his own name, him will ye receive."

In verse 11, John saw a second beast of the earth, the false prophet who will complete Satan's hellish, unholy trinity. John saw this beast rise up; it had two horns like a lamb, and it spoke like a dragon. The anti-Christ will be a Gentile, while the false prophet will be Jewish. Remember that the anti-Christ will rise up from the sea of humanity, or the Gentile nations, while the false prophet will rise out of the earth. This is in stark contrast to Christ, who was sent to earth from heaven (Isaiah 7:14, 9:6–7; John 1:14; Galatians 4:4).
The second beast is different from the first, which had ten horns, symbolic of the European Union nations. The second beast had two horns, like a lamb. This refers to its counterfeit office and not to Jesus Christ, our great High Priest from God who offered Himself as a sacrifice for our sins (John 1:19; Colossians 2:13–14; 1 John 2:2).

The ten horns of the first beast represent the political power of the anti-Christ, while the two horns of the second beast represent the spiritual power of the false prophet. The dragon, Satan, gives his power to the first beast and his spirit to the second beast, which speaks like a dragon. These horns are idealism, world philosophy, materialism, pantheism, and atheism or are simply a form of godliness that denies the power thereof (2 Timothy 3:1–7).

Satan has given the world a virtual buffet of religions to choose from beginning at the Tower of Babel with Nimrod. Religion brings a soul into captivity and will send a soul straight to hell. Only the grace of God by faith alone in Jesus Christ can set the captive free and save a soul (Isaiah 14:16–17).

There is great biblical evidence that the false prophet will be Jewish when Scripture is compared to Scripture and to the culture and customs of the Jewish religion and national history.

God's prophets throughout the ages have declared Israel's four besetting sins. It is important to remember that not only nations have besetting sins but also individuals and families that are **generational curses.** What parents do in moderation, the children and following generations will do in excess, including indulging in alcohol, drugs, immorality, pornography, adultery, divorce, and suicide.

What are America's besetting sins? Greed, materialism, and rampant viewing of pornography on the Internet and TV. Since the 1973 *Roe v. Wade* Supreme Court decision, over 64 million innocent babies have been murdered in Planned Parenthood's abortion chop shops in America. We are a nation consumed by addictions to pleasure, illegal drugs, and the abuse of prescription drugs on all levels of society. Alcoholism is a major contributing factor in the general physical decline in health of American society; the cost of treating it is in the billions of dollars each year. The most recent national curse has become the nation's fascination with the occult and the debate on same-sex marriage and civil unions. This is the lust of the eye, the lust of the flesh, and the pride of life (1 John 2:15–17).

The book of Judges reveals Israel's cycles of sin and its people's besetting sins, including idolatry (Exodus 32:1–4) as told in the narrative of Aaron and the golden calf idol, immorality (Genesis 38:1–16) in the narrative of Judah and Tamar, adultery (2 Samuel 11:1–8) in the sin of David and Bathsheba, and the oppression of the poor and the perversion of justice in the nation (Ezekiel 18:1–12).

In Ezekiel 8:5–18, God gave us the graphic example of Israel's perverted worship by the priest in the house of the Lord. Israel was worshipping creatures and idols in Ezekiel's vision of Jerusalem before the judgment of the Lord with the slaughter and captivity of the nation.

The false prophet will also pervert worship and demand sacrifices and allegiance to the image of the beast that the anti-Christ will erect in the tribulation temple in Jerusalem.

Who resisted God, the Word of God, and the prophet of God in the Old Testament? The priest of the temple (Acts 7:52). Who resisted and consented to the death of Stephen? The priest of the temple (Acts 7:54–60). Who resisted, persecuted, slandered, and assaulted Jesus Christ and ultimately had Christ crucified? The priests, Pharisees, Sadducees, Scribes and the Jewish religious leaders of that day. This false prophet will also resist Christ and His saints and pervert worship in the temple and the nation. The false prophet, the beast of the earth who speaks like a dragon, will be Jewish.

In verses 12 through 15, we read that the false prophet will attempt to mimic the Holy Spirit of God; he will be the third person of the hellish trinity. The Holy Spirit of God leads people to truth (John 14:17), while the false prophet will seduce them into error (Revelation 13:11, 14). The Holy Spirit glorifies Christ Jesus (John 16:13), while the false prophet glorifies the anti-Christ (Revelation 13:12). The Holy Spirit made fire come down from heaven on Pentecost (Acts 2:3), while the false prophet will do likewise on earth in view of people as a counterfeit miracle. The Holy Spirit gives life (Romans 8:2), while the false prophet kills (Revelation 13:15). The Holy Spirit marks with a seal of the Living God all who belong to the Lord by faith in Christ Jesus (Ephesians 1:13), while the false prophet marks those who worship Satan with the **mark of the beast, 666.**
The image of the beast, **the abomination of desecration** from Daniel 9:27 and Matthew 24:15, will be set in the tribulation temple in Jerusalem, and humanity will worship the image of the beast. It is noteworthy how much people desire worship; that is seen today as never before in music, videos, Hollywood award ceremonies, in the pomp of the State of the Union address every January, and in the **demigod worship** of our athletes. But this is nothing new; the Bible recounts numerous occasions when people demanded worship. Nebuchadnezzar's dream of the golden image in Daniel 3 is an example, as is the fiery furnace. Darius decreed that only he could be prayed to in Daniel 6. And historically, it is seen in the

anti-Christ typology of Antiochus Epiphanes, who conquered Jerusalem and set images of pagan gods in the temple and slaughtered and sacrificed a sow and desecrated the sacred altar.

The anti-Christ will receive power to speak and act. It is important to understand that **magic is not a miracle.** When Moses appeared before Pharaoh to demand the release of the Hebrews by the command of God, Moses gave a sign; he turned Aaron's staff into a serpent. The magicians in Pharaoh's court, Jannes and Jambres, did the same by the power of the black arts, occult magic. The staff of Moses digested their serpents as recorded in Exodus 7:11–20, and Paul quoted this in his letter to Timothy in 2 Timothy 3:8–9.

In verses 16 through 18, we read that the **mark of the beast** will be used by the false prophet to identify the followers of the anti-Christ during this period of the tribulation. The Scripture informs us he will cause all to take the m**ark of the beast on** their right hands or foreheads. Without the mark of the beast, no one will be able to buy or sell. This is a mark of ownership, the mark of a slave.

Some say the mark will be a computer chip implanted into the right hand or forehead with a code similar to the universal bar coding system used in retail stores at checkout. This chip, however, would contain personal identification information. We know the beast only by his description at this time as the man of sin, the son of perdition, the evil one, the destroyer, or the anti-Christ, but the text is clear and indicates he will have a real name. I find it interesting and frightening that one of the great characteristics of our present **terminal generation** is tattoos; the Bible specifically prohibits the marking of our flesh.

The mark may possibly be the number 666, which identifies the beast and the property of the beast as slave worshippers by the tattoo on the right hand or forehead. The danger of bearing this mark is in Revelation 19:20.

> The beast was taken, and with him the false prophet that
> wrought miracles before him, with which he deceived
> them that had received the mark of the beast, and them

that worshipped his image. These both were cast [alive] into a lake of fire burning with brimstone.

What does 666 mean? This subject has had many varied and silly interpretations throughout the ages. Some have arranged the numbers according to the Hebrew, Greek, and Latin alphabets and arrived at such names as Nero, Muhammad, the pope, Napoleon, and even Hitler. The Bible is silent on the definition of this number, but it speaks prophetically about the number with numerous examples. The number 6 is the number of man, and the number 7 is God's number of perfection. This carries us back to the Old Testament and Daniel's prophecy, when Nebuchadnezzar demanded a golden statue be erected in his honor; all had to pray to the idol or face death in a furnace. The statue erected was sixty cubits high by six cubits wide and overlaid with gold. The mathematics of this dimension work out as 666. The creation of humanity was on the sixth day, and all of man's achievements will always fall short of God's perfection.

The Lamb and the 144,000: Revelation 14

1. The Lamb and the 144,000—14:1–5
2. The angel with the everlasting gospel—14:6–7
3. The fall of Babylon announced—14:8
4. The doom of the beast worshippers announced—14:9–12
5. The blessedness of the holy dead—14:13
6. The vision of Armageddon—14:14–20

Revelation 14 is another intermission chapter; it reveals the final events that will occur at the end of the great tribulation. This is the final intermission in Revelation, and it separates the trumpet judgments, the woe judgments from the coming vial judgments. The seven years of the great tribulation are quickly coming to a close, and the Christ's Second Advent is on the horizon.

In verses 1 through 5, John saw the Lamb of God, Jesus Christ, standing on Mount Sion, Greek for "Zion" and one of the several names for Mount Hermon from Deuteronomy 4:48. Jesus had left the throne of heaven to rapture and reclaim the 144,000 faithful witnesses who were sealed with the name of God the Father and Jesus the Son on their foreheads from chapter 7. It is important to note the protection of God on their lives and the power of the seal of God; not one sealed saint would be lost during their ministry in the tribulation.

John heard the Holy Spirit speak from heaven, and he heard the harps of the saints. The saints had their harps back, and there was great joy (Psalm 137:2). John heard the 144,000 sing a new song that was possibly mentioned in Psalm 57. They sang before the four angelic creatures above the throne and before the twenty-four elders of Revelation 4. It was a song of the redemption and glory to God for His mercy and protection.

John described the 144,000 as unmarried virgin men sanctified of God who followed the Lamb wherever He led them. They were redeemed by God and without guile for they were without fault before the throne of God. Simply the promise of God to the faithful from Romans 5:1, and 8:1 to be apart from the wrath of God, and to have peace with God, and without condemnation.

We have no fear or doubt of God's power and ability to rapture the saint or to raise the dead to life; the Bible evidence for this is overwhelming. Enoch walked with God, and he was not, for God took him. The prophet Elijah was caught up to heaven in the chariot of God as witnessed by Elisha. The widow of Nain had her son raised to life during his funeral procession. The twelve-year-old young maiden Jesus called, Lazarus the friend of Jesus was resurrected on the fourth day as was seen by his sisters Martha and Mary and by a crowd at the tomb. On the third day, Jesus Christ rose from the grave and was seen by the women, the apostles, the disciples, and by a crowd of over 500 as recorded by Luke. According to Revelation 4:1, a day is coming for this **terminal generation** when Jesus Christ will call up His church in the rapture.

In verses 6 and 7, John saw and heard another angel that flew in the midst of heaven, our atmosphere, announcing the everlasting gospel to all souls on earth, to every nation, kindred, tongue, and people. Through His great mercy and compassion, God wants all people come to repentance and to be saved; God is no respecter of persons (Acts 10:34).

The angel announces the everlasting gospel and the commands to fear God (Ecclesiastes 12:13), give glory to God for judgment was coming soon (the hour of His judgment), and worship the Creator of all things.

The Greek word *gospel* translates as "**good news,**" and there are four forms of the gospel in Scripture.

1. The **gospel of the kingdom,** the good news of God's purpose to set up on earth His kingdom in fulfillment of the Davidic covenant (2 Samuel 7:16).
2. The **gospel of the grace of God, which** is the preaching of the good news of Jesus Christ, the Son of God, who was the rejected King who suffered, died, and rose again on the third day according to Scripture (1 Corinthians 15:1–4).
3. The e**verlasting gospel,** the good news preached to the earth and all inhabitants by an angel of God at the end of the tribulation period. This includes the announcements of the coming judgments from Matthew 25:31; it is a message of good news to Israel and those who survived the great tribulation.
4. That which Paul the apostle calls "my gospel" (Romans 2:6), the grace of God that not only forgives and saves sinners but also gives the revelation of His will as shown in 2 Peter 3:8–9.

There is another gospel, the **Gnostic gospel that** Paul the apostle warned of in 2 Corinthians 11:4 and Galatians 1:6. The Gnostic gospel is a perversion and corruption of the good news that Jesus Christ rose bodily from the grave on the third day. There are several books available today that explain the Gnostic gospel or promote the lies written therein. The Gnostic gospel was founded on the notion that Jesus Christ was not the incarnate Son of God but came only in the Spirit. Therefore, Christ did not really die on the cross but only appeared to have died, and the resurrection was just a reappearing of His Spirit.

The Gnostics advanced the notion that there were many paths to salvation and that Christ alone could not save or keep anyone. According to Gnosticism, you must labor to save yourself by works of righteousness.

In verse 8, John saw a second angel that proclaimed the fall of Babylon because she seduces the world to commit fornication (brazen immorality, hostility toward God and the saints). God will return to her the wine of wrath. This passage is prophetic and parenthetical to Revelation 17 and 18, when religious Babylon and commercial Babylon were destroyed.

Today, billions of dollars are being poured into the city on the Tigris and Euphrates Rivers. No doubt, this will result in the worst financial investment in the twenty-first century, as this city will be destroyed in one hour. The location and details of the reconstruction of Babylon will be covered more fully in Revelation 18.

In verses 9 through 12, John saw a third angel announcing the doom of the beast worshippers, those who received the **mark of the beast, 666.** Those who followed Satan received the wrath of God without measure, or better translated as "not diluted but full strength," and it was poured out on them in the **vial judgments** to follow. The lake of fire and eternal separation from God would be their final destination; they would suffer along with all beast worshippers.

From the language of verses 10–11, we begin to understand the horror and terror of hell. It is a physical location of eternal hopelessness, loss, and torment. Those there will have eternal regrets for their decisions to serve Satan rather than repent and receive the salvation of Jesus Christ.

Hell will be the final judgment upon the anti-Christ, the false prophet, the fallen angels, and Satan. Hell will be the final destination from which there is no pardon for any who lived unrighteous lives apart from Christ. The Word says, "The smoke of their torment rose up forever and ever; and they have no rest day or night." Yes, hell is real. It is an abiding place but not a resting place. There is not a doctrine of annihilation found in the Bible, and the Word of God is clear: heaven is eternal, everlasting joy for the saint, while hell is eternal, everlasting punishment and torment for the unrepentant sinner. We must understand that Satan will not rule in hell; he will be tormented and suffer for eternity!

In verse 12, the perseverance of the saints is explained and defined: they kept the Commandments and by faith accepted Jesus Christ as their Lord and Savior; they were thus freed from the wrath of God and knelt before Him without condemnation.

In verse 13, the Holy Spirit told John to write, "Blessed are the dead that die in the Lord, from hence-forth; yea saith the Spirit, that they may rest from their labors, and their works do follow them" (Hebrews 4:1–11). Hebrews 11 is the great faith chapter in the Bible and the great chapter on rest! The rest of God for the saint is not soul sleep but a perfect, conscious rest, not sleepless nights; all is a peace, and there is joy unspeakable and full of glory in Christ Jesus.

When it comes to "their works followed them" in this verse, we must be careful how we work and labor in this life. We are told to lay up our treasures in heaven. Are you working on the right things? Are your treasures in heaven, or will they all be left behind? Will you be proud of the works that follow you as you stand before the bema seat of Christ to give an account of your service and works, or will you be ashamed? The **bema seat of Christ is where Christians, saved folks, stand.** We are not before Christ's seat to give an account of our souls but to be rewarded with crowns or experience loss for poor service to the Lord as Christians.

In verses 14 through 20, John saw the vision of Armageddon, the final battle in the great tribulation but not the final battle of time. This has often been referred to as Ezekiel's war (Ezekiel 38–39).

John did not see all the battle, but he saw the Son of God coming in the clouds (Acts 1:8–11), and an angel cried for Christ to thrust in His sickle and harvest the earth. Two more avenging angels came from heaven to judge the inhabitants of earth. The illustration was one of gathering grapes for harvest and being cast into the wine press of God.

The battle will not take place in Jerusalem but outside the city. The carnage of this gory feast of the Lord for the kings and armies that come down to invade Israel for spoil and plunder will result in a horrifying blood bath of 200 million. The river of blood from the carnage based on the Bible's use of the word *furlong* will be 160 miles long and four to five feet deep. This pool of stagnant, coagulating blood of dead people will flow down the Valley of Megiddo.

More will be said about Ezekiel's war later in this study, but this is the feast the Lord prepared for sin, and Ezekiel recorded that it would take seven months to bury all the dead and seven years to burn all the instruments of war. No trees will be cut for firewood for seven years.

Part VIII

The Seven Vial or Bowl Judgments: Revelation Chapters 15–16

1. The vision of the seven last plagues; the vials of the wrath of God—15:1–8
2. The first vial, grievous sores—16:1–2
3. The second vial, the sea turned to blood—16:3
4. The third vial, the fresh water turned to blood—16:4–7
5. The fourth vial, people scorched with intense heat—16:8–9
6. The fifth vial, darkness upon the earth—16:10–11
7. The sixth vial, the River Euphrates dried up—16:12–16
8. The seventh vial, a voice from heaven, "It is done"—16:17–21

Revelation 15, the shortest chapter in the book, presents John's vision of the seven last plagues and vial judgments of God on sinful humanity. John saw seven angels with seven vials containing the wrath of God. The vial judgments were more intense than the seal, trumpet, or woe judgments, and they all happened in rapid succession. It is important to know and understand the reason for the intensity and rapidity of these judgments; the answer is in Revelation 9:20–21: humanity repented not of its sins.

In verse 1, John saw another great and wonderful sign, seven angels with the seven last plagues in vials filled with the wrath of God.

Every attribute of God, both His communicable and incommunicable attributes, are the highest perfection of holiness. Holiness is the greatest description of God, and all of God's other divine characteristics reflect upon His holiness in grace, mercy, righteousness, power, wisdom, strength, justice, and wrath. The holiness of God demands justice for the righteous saint and punishment for the unrepentant sinner.

Adam and Eve were driven from Eden, from the Tree of Life, by the mercy of God to prevent them from living forever in sin. The progress and spread of sin throughout humanity resulted in the judgment of the flood. Man's rebellion against God continued with the building of the Tower of Babel and the cruel leadership of Nimrod; in response, God confused the languages and scattered the nations. All this occurred in just the first six generation of humanity as recorded in the first eleven chapters of the Bible.

The Bible is a book about our Redeemer; it is Christocentric from Genesis to Revelation, but woven into its pages are accounts of the human race from Creation to Revelation. The Bible is also a book of the rebellion of Satan and a third of the angelic host and of men. If it were not for the grace of God, none would survive. John 3:36 reveals one of the great truths and promises of the Bible: "He that believeth on the Son, hath everlasting life, and he that believeth not on the Son hath not life and the wrath of God abideth on him." This freedom from the wrath of God is affirmed in the writings of Paul the apostle in Romans 5:1: "Therefore being justified by faith we have peace with God, through our Lord Jesus Christ." Amen!

John saw heaven's glory and its citizens in verses 2 through 4 and noted four things.

1. A sea that looked like glass mingled with fire, reminiscent of the light paintings of the late great artist Thomas Kinkade, the painter of light.
2. Saints who refused the mark of the beast.
3. Saints standing on the sea that looked like glass mingled with fire. They were no longer bound by natural laws; they were able to experience and enjoy the supernatural by standing on water. The apostle Peter walked on the Sea of Galilee, and the saints of God stood on the crystal sea. This truly will be a beautiful thing to behold in glory.
4. Saints singing the song of Moses from Exodus 15:1 and the song of the Lamb from Psalm 22:22.

John heard the declaration of the saints of God: great and marvelous were God's works, God was the Almighty God, God was just and true in all His ways, and He was the King of all the saints. The saints asked a rhetorical question, "Who shall not fear thee or better reverence thee and glorify thy name?" "For thou only art holy: for all nations shall come and worship before thee." This fulfills the prophecy in Isaiah 66:19–24, when all nations would come and worship God and Christ during the millennium and for eternity. Angels and people saw the judgments of God.

In verses 5 through 8, John saw the temple of God opened in the third heaven, God's abode. Seven angels came out of the temple with the seven last plagues of the tribulation. They were clothed in pure white linen and wore golden girdles. One of the four living angelic creatures gave the seven angels the seven vials of the wrath of God.

The temple was filled with smoke from the glory of God and from His power (Isaiah 6:1–8; Exodus 25:9, 40; Hebrews 8:2, 5, 9:24; Revelation 14:15, 17, 16:1, 17). And no one could enter the temple until the seven last plagues were completed. This may explain why the choir was standing on the sea of glass. God mercifully removed and shielded His saints from His judgments. God shielded the Hebrews from the plagues on Egypt and the passing of the death angel through Egypt. God shielded Moses in the cleft of the rock, and He shielded the Hebrews in their wilderness wanderings with a cloud and a pillar of fire.

Revelation 16:1–21

John heard the voice of Jesus Christ commanding the seven angels to pour out their vials of wrath upon the earth in verse 1. These judgments happened in rapid succession and resulted in the gathering of the armies of the world's nations against Israel in the Valley of Megiddo, which means **"place of the crowds."** Megiddo is six miles from Mount Carmel and eleven miles from Nazareth on the southern rim of the Esdraelon Plain. There have been many historic battles fought in this valley and plain; Napoleon said, "It is a perfect battle ground." (Read Joshua 12:21, 2 Kings 23:29, and 2 Chronicles 35:22–24 for the history of these battles).

In verse 2, the first angel poured out his vial on earth, and a noisome and grievous sore fell upon all those who had taken the mark of the beast. God's wrath poured out on the rebellious with the mark of Satan, and God's mercy poured out on the righteous (Exodus 9:8–12). The word *noisome* translates as "evil," "incurable"; it serves as a reflection of the rebellious person's character and nature, *kakos, worthless. Grievous* translates as hurtful in effect and influence, and *ponerois, to make one derelict.*

In verse 3, the second angel poured out his vial, and all saltwater was turned to blood, and every creature in the sea died. The stench will be unbearable, and all sea travel will cease. In verse 4, the third angel poured out his vial, and all fresh water was turned to blood, and deaths resulted from dehydration.

Verses 5 through 7 include the testimony of this angel, whom God assigned as the superintendent of the waters of the earth. Remember the angels of the wind and weather assigned by God in Revelation 7:1. The testimony of the angel was that God was righteous, God was eternal, God judged righteously because sinful people shed the blood of the saints and the prophets, God gave them blood to drink, and God's judgments were true and righteous.

As you read this portion of the tribulation judgments, you may consider storing up fresh water, but that will not help! *All* in biblical Greek is *paz*; this means that all water, even that in cisterns or bottles, will yield only blood. You must repent immediately and receive Jesus Christ as your personal Savior; that way, you will never experience the terror and suffering of the great tribulation. The Bible example of this is found in the judgments of God on Egypt; the Scripture is clear—there was no water to drink in all of Egypt (Exodus 7:20–25).

In verses 8 and 9, John saw dramatic climate changes as the fourth angel poured out his vial on the sun to scorch people with fire, solar flares, and intensified UV rays that caused sunburns, but this judgment will be more severe, intense, and debilitating.

Because of this, humanity should repent of its sin, but people instead will blaspheme the name of God and refuse to repent and not give God the glory. How many people today have wallowed in their sins, transgressions, and iniquities and suffered needlessly for years and only cursed and blamed God? Many!

There are four Bible-based reasons for bad things to happen to good people, to put it in modern vernacular.

1. People suffer because of their sins as punishment from God. Psalm 51:1–15 captures the sin of David with Bathsheba, his repentance, and his request to return the joy of salvation to him. We must not jump to conclusions when we see a saint suffering trials and afflictions. All suffering is not the result of personal sin; if it is, God always informs the person of the sin, the punishment, and the reason first.

2. People suffer for righteousness' sake. There is a great example in the Bible narratives of the prophets, disciples, and apostles who suffered for the cause of Christ in righteousness; they will receive martyrs' crowns from Christ.

3. People suffer for the prevention of a greater sin as seen in the example of the apostle Paul who prayed three times for the thorn in his flesh to be removed. Possibly, the suffering was related to an eye disease or from the many torturous beatings and stonings he had endured. But the Lord told Paul that His grace was sufficient, and Paul understood that the affliction helped him stay humble before the Lord in ministry (2 Corinthians 12:1–10).

4. People suffer for the glory of God. Probably, the most difficult of the four reasons for suffering for people to understand is that God is glorified through our suffering. In John 9:1–41, we read of the man born blind. As Jesus and the disciples passed by him, the disciples asked Jesus, "Who did sin, this man or his parents that he was born blind?" Jesus responded that neither the man nor his parents had sinned, that he had been born blind so that the works of God—grace and glory—should be manifest in him. Under the laws of the Pharisees, people with afflictions were condemned as having sinned in the womb, or the parents were guilty, and the infirmity was a judgment from God. This is wrong, according to Jesus. He healed the blind man, the power of God was manifested in his life, and the Lord was glorified. The man at the end of the story received Jesus Christ as his Savior, and the grace of God was upon him. It would surely be better to enter heaven blind than to go to hell with twenty-twenty vision (Mark 9:47).

In verses 10 and 11, John saw the fifth angel with the fifth vial, and darkness was poured out upon the earth (Joel 2:30–32), fulfilling the Old Testament minor prophet's words. As the sun grew darker, it got hotter, and this darkness was poured out on Satan's seat, and very appropriately since Satan is the Prince of Darkness.

Satan's seat at this point in the great tribulation will be in Jerusalem, which will become the center of worldwide Satanic worship in the tribulation temple with the image of the beast set in the Holy of Holies, desecrating the temple altar. This darkness will encompass the world because of the sins of humanity experienced by the world during the last three hours of Christ's life. Colossians 2:13–14 tell us that Christ took all the sins of humanity from the beginning until the end of time and nailed the handwriting of the ordinance against us to His cross. It was the custom of the Roman government when a criminal was condemned to death to write the guilty verdict on parchment along with the crime and the criminal's name for all to see. Christ took our guilty verdict and nailed it to His tree. What a ghastly mental picture—Christ's cross covered with countless billons of humanity's guilty verdicts.

The blood of the Lamb shed for us by Jesus on the cross overcame the darkness of sin as Jesus Christ drank our cup of iniquity. Luke 23:44–45 records that from the sixth to the ninth hour of Christ's crucifixion, darkness was over all the earth, the sun was darkened by the sweep of sin. Secular history records that an unnatural darkness not the result of a solar eclipse covered the entire known earth as recorded in the letters from Rome to Pontius Pilate in Jerusalem.

The result of the fifth vial judgment of darkness on sinful humanity tells us that people will gnaw their tongues because of the pain and the sores (v. 2), and they will blaspheme God and not repent of their deeds. God used painful sores and boils in His judgments upon rebellion and sin when He afflicted Pharaoh and Egypt for the release of the Hebrews. God struck people, including Uzziah, Gehazi, and Miriam, with leprosy.

In verse 12, John saw the sixth angel pour out the sixth vial on the Euphrates River, drying it and making a path for the armies and kings of the north to descend on Israel. With this, God's rattrap was sprung on Satan, the anti-Christ, the false prophet, and all who worshipped the beast and his image.

The Euphrates is 1,800 miles long, 3,600 feet wide, and 30 feet deep in most places and separates the East from the West as a natural barrier to invasion. This area is also the cradle of civilization, and it will become the grave for 200 million.

Verses 13 through 16 are parenthetical; they amplify what John saw of the Battle of Armageddon. God was gathering the armies of the north to the Valley of Megiddo. Satan unleashed three unclean spirits described by John as frogs; these evil fallen angels had the ability to organize an army from the kings of the earth and the whole world in an attempt to destroy Israel, and this was the anti-Christ's futile attempt to stay in power. Jesus Christ said, "I come quickly, like a thief in the night"; He gathered armies numbering more than 200 million in the valley of death and destruction, Megiddo, translated in Hebrew as "Armageddon."

In verses 17 through 21, the seventh angel poured out the seventh vial, and John heard three great statements. "It is done!" The other time this statement was used in the Bible was in John 19:20; it recorded one of the seven cries of Christ from the cross. He said, "It is done!" He meant that salvation's plan was finished, sin had been paid in full, and sin had been forgiven by His shed blood sacrifice. In 1 John 2:2 and 2 Corinthians 5:2 are explanations of the breadth, depth, and expanse of Christ's sacrifice for repentant sinners. We give thanks today that Jesus Christ cried out, "It is done" and not, "It is started." There is nothing we can do for the forgiveness of our sins or our salvation but to receive the gift of God in our lives by faith alone in the finished work of Christ.

The world's greatest earthquake happened when the seventh vial was poured out on the earth; it truly shook the foundations of the world, and all other earthquakes will pale in comparison to this judgment's magnitude. The earthquake will level great cities of the world, destroy every island, including Japan, Australia, Greenland, England, Ireland, Iceland, Hawaii, and all those on every coast of every continent. In the

Olivet Discourse, Jesus instructed the disciples of the signs of the end time for the **terminal generation, including earthquakes in diverse places.**

The world's greatest hailstorm will fall upon unrepentant humanity. These hailstones will weigh 125 pounds and will slay many. This hail has been on reserve in heaven since antiquity; in Job 38:21–23, God asked Job, "Hast thou seen the treasures of the snow and hail laid up in store against the Day of Judgment?" This affirms the omniscience of God in all matters.

Global weather runs in cycles, but this past year, the judgment of snow upon the most unusual and extensive areas of the United States was most uncommon; the nation suffered a prolonged and cold winter and much snow.

The Seven Dooms of Babylon: Revelation 17–18

1. Religious Babylon doomed—17:1–18
2. Commercial Babylon doomed—18:1–24
3. God's view of Babylon, the human view, and the angelic view—17–18

Revelation 17 and 18 are two of the more difficult chapters in this study. In Revelation 17, Babylon was a geographic location, but it was also symbolic of the one-world apostate religious system that dates to Genesis 11:1–9 and the **Tower of Babel,** whose name translates as "**confusion.**" Nimrod and his wife, Semerimus, served as the evil, satanic leadership of this one-world religion and ascribed worship to their son, Tammuz. It is from this evil family that the course of Satan's religion may be traced through the ages. The *great whore of Babylon* is symbolic of the faithless and perverse apostate church in the last days. The illustration of the great whore was used in the Old and the New Testaments to describe a false religion.

Religious Babylon will come to power at the beginning of the tribulation period, when the anti-Christ receives the position and power as leader of the **new world order, a phrase** used repeatedly by the world's political leaders since the nineteenth century. Presidents have used it in their inauguration addresses and in the formation of the United Nations. The **New Deal is nothing more than Satan's original plan for his great society, just repackaged with a new name!**

Religious Babylon will be destroyed by the anti-Christ when Satan commands through the false prophet that all nations and people must worship his image of the beast in the rebuilt tribulation temple in Jerusalem.

Revelation 18 deals with commercial Babylon, which will control the global economy in every aspect during the tribulation era. Commercial Babylon will swiftly come into power following the rapture of the church and the rise of the anti-Christ during the seven years of his brief rule over the world. Commercial Babylon will be destroyed in one day by the Second Advent of Jesus Christ with the rebellion of the armies of the world defeated in the Valley of Megiddo during the Battle of Armageddon (Revelation 16:9).

Revelation 17 and 18 reveal a story within a story much like a mystery novel. From the previous pages in the study, we know Satan will empower the anti-Christ and the false prophet to consolidate Satan's power in Jerusalem as a counterfeit ascension of Christ to power in the Second Advent. During the same time, a one-world religion will rise from the *revived Roman Empire,* and Satan will tolerate this for three and a half years through a peace treaty brokered by the anti-Christ with Israel and the rebuilding of the tribulation temple in Jerusalem. At the midpoint of the tribulation, Satan will destroy this ecumenical movement when it tries to assume the position of worldwide religious worship. Theologians have speculated about the identity of this one-world religion. Based on Revelation 17:1–7, many believe this one-world religion rising out of the *revived Roman Empire* will be the Roman Catholic Church and the papacy. It is my opinion that this position is not consistent when prophetic Scripture is compared to Scripture that will be presented from the exegesis of Revelation 17:9. It is my understanding that Rome will not be the center of the world's religious worship, that it will be Israel, specifically Jerusalem, where Satan's seat will be, where the anti-Christ and the false prophet will dwell, and where the tribulation temple will be reconstructed.

The anti-Christ will destroy religious Babylon by detesting the harlot church, then despoiling her, then disgracing her, then devouring her, and finally destroying her. Satan will destroy his competition for praise and worship. Satan's world religion historic time line will be included in this chapter.

In Revelation 17 and 18, the *revived Roman Empire* embodied the worst traits of the Babylonian, Medo-Persian, Greek, and Roman Empires as described by the prophet Daniel in his beast vision in Daniel 7–8.

In Revelation 17:1, John saw a vision he could not comprehend until one of the seven angels with the vial judgments revealed to him the mystery judgment of the **great whore, who** represented the faithless, perverse apostate world church (vv. 17:7, 9, 15). This one-world religion was described as a powerful and sinful harlot that comprised millions from all the world's religions under the banner of one-world religion, the *present ecumenical movement of the terminal generation,* which is growing in our present day. Verse 1 tells us that the *harlot* sits upon many waters, from the Gentile nations and the *revived Roman Empire, and from numerous denominations today,* and her influence will be worldwide.

The influence of this one-world religion will no doubt make the front cover of magazines and be the topic of discussion on news channels. Its influence will corrupt the earth by drawing many into a false sense of religious security.

In verse 3, the angel carried John in the Spirit, as noted in Revelation 21:10, Matthew 1:18, and Acts 2:4, into the wilderness. John saw a woman sitting on a scarlet beast (Revelation 12:3) from the seven-personages passage, and the beast was full of names of blasphemy (Revelation 13:1) and had seven heads and ten horns. This identifies the scarlet beast as the anti-Christ empowered by Satan, the source of the woman's apostate church worship. In verse 4, she was the one-world church that possessed unlimited wealth and power over humanity. She had a name on her forehead in verse 5, and in John's day, it was a common practice of prostitutes to wear their names in jewelry on their foreheads to advertise their trade and immorality, perversion, adultery, and corruption.

In verse 6, she was described as being drunk with the blood of the saints. Only history will reveal how many saints and the followers of Jesus Christ have been tortured, imprisoned, and executed in the name of religion. *Foxe's Book of Martyrs* presents historically those slain for the cause of Christ and the Word of God. A current magazine, *The Voice of the Martyr*, contains the names and stories of those suffering for the cause of Christ around the world. Censure and hatred for Christians in America is on the rise, and our nation is growing more tolerant of social, moral, and ethical sins and less tolerant of the Word of God, the name of Jesus Christ, and our Christian values founded on the Word of God. Very soon, Christians in America will have their names listed on the martyrs' rolls for holding fast to truth and declaring the Word of God to a sin-sick, dying world.

In verse 7, the mystery of the woman is revealed to John as the *harlot apostate world religion teamed up with the anti-Christ, the beast of Revelation 17:3, 7.* In verse 8, we learn that the last form of the Gentile world power, the *revived Roman Empire* from Nebuchadnezzar's dream vision and Daniel 2:42, 7–9 and religious Babylon, will deceive the nations by her perverted worship, whose rise to power was from the very depths of hell, and the world will not recognize this woman or this false world religion for what it really is until it is too late. Only those whose names are in the Lamb's Book of Life have the spirit of discernment and the knowledge of the Word of God to test the spirits. In 1 John 4:1–4, the Word tells us to "know that every spirit that does not confess the incarnation of the Son of God, the deity of Jesus Christ is not from God, but has the spirit of the anti-Christ dwelling in them."

Verse 9 is both symbolic and historical; it refers to the seven kingdoms, not to a specific geographical location. Some speculate that Rome will be the city because it is surrounded by seven hills and the emperors wore robes of purple and scarlet (17:4). Upon closer examination of Scripture, however, the location of religious Babylon will most likely be Jerusalem, where Satan's seat will be during the tribulation. Verse 18 identifies the "great city which reigneth over the kings of the earth." In Revelation 11:8, we read, "Their dead bodies shall lie in the street of that Great City, which spiritually is called Sodom and Egypt, where our Lord was crucified." Jesus Christ was crucified in Jerusalem, not Rome.

Verse 10 requires us to look deeply into Bible history. The seven heads were the seven mountains, and the seven nations were kings. John wrote that five had fallen, one was, and one was not yet. This is most significant in understanding this passage and key to the city location.

In Revelation 1, John was instructed to write the past, present, and future. This verse is from the memory of John concerning the past and his present and future understanding as revealed prophetically by the Spirit of God to John.

The seven nations are the once-powerful empires of Egypt, Assyria, Babylon, Medo-Persia, Greece, Rome, and the revived Roman Empire. This accounts for the seven nations symbolically seen as seven hills or mountains consistent with Daniel's beast visions. The one nation that was during John's time was the Roman Empire. The one nation yet to come is the revived Roman Empire, which will be revealed in place and in power following the rapture of the church.

In verse 11, the beast, the anti-Christ, is the one currently not revealed as a world leader in our terminal generation; he will rise following the rapture (2 Thessalonians 2:1–12). The anti-Christ will be the eighth ruler, and his rise to power will come out of the *revived Roman Empire and the European League of Nations.* Today, there are thirteen nations in the European Union three will fall through diplomacy of the anti-Christ when he comes to power.

Verses 12 through 15 describe how quickly these ten kings will come to power with the beast. They will be unified in mind and purpose (v. 13), give their support to Satan (v. 13), and will make war with the Lamb. The Lord will overcome them at Armageddon when their armies march on Jerusalem.

In verse 15, the angel explained to John the water on which the *whore sat was* religious Babylon, which comprised people, multitudes, nations, tongues, and the whole earth in rebellion against God.

In verses 16 through 18, God used the anti-Christ to destroy this false world religion and thereby fulfilled God's will until the Word of God was fulfilled entirely according to prophecy.

Satan's Historic World Religion Time Line

Satan's desire to control worship began when He rebelled against God (Isaiah 14; Ezekiel 28). His church began historically at the **Tower of Babel** (Genesis 11:1–9), which was close to the garden of Eden. This first religion was for the purpose of worshipping the god of this world, Satan.

Nimrod, Noah's wicked and apostate grandson, was Satan's first minister (Genesis 10:8–10). Secular history records that Nimrod married **Semerimus,** who was as evil and demonic as **Nimrod.** Their first son, **Tammuz, was** the first typology of the anti-Christ. Semerimus instituted a religious system that made her and her son objects of divine worship. The city of Babylon was the seat of Satan worship until it fell in 536 BC to the Persians.

This religion spread from Babylon to Phoenicia under the name of **Ashteroth** and **Tammuz.** From Phoenicia, it traveled to Pergamos in Asia Minor (Revelation 2:13, "where Satan has his seat"). In Egypt, the cult was known as **Isia and Horus.** In Greece, it became known as **Aphrodite and Eros.** In Rome, the mother and child cult was worshipped as **Venus and Cupid.** In China, it became known as **Mother Shing Moo and her child.**

This satanic church worshipped Semerimus as the **queen of heaven who** alone would administer salvation; her son, Tammuz, was slain and rose on the fortieth day, in celebration of which an annual feast was held. Colored eggs were exchanged and eaten as a sign of his resurrection. An evergreen tree was to be displayed in the homes during the feast. Then hotcakes with the letter "T" on them were baked and eaten. **Notice anything here**

unusual? The pagan Christmas and Easter traditions were perverted by Satan.

But God calls us to righteousness and warns of idolatry (Joshua 24:2–3). In 2000 BC, God called Abraham from idolatry and to the promised land. By the ninth century BC, Israel had returned to idol worship under the name **Baal.**

Ezekiel and Jeremiah warned of this hellish worship. Ezekiel (8:14) wrote, "Then he brought me to the door of the LORD's house which was toward the north, and behold, there sat women weeping for **Tammuz.**" Jeremiah wrote (7:18, 44:25), "The children gather wood, and the father kindles the fire, and the women knead their dough, to make cakes to the **Queen of Heaven,** to burn incense to the **Queen of Heaven**, to pour out drink offerings unto her."

By the time of Christ's ministry, this cult had so influenced Roman life that the Caesars were not only crowned the emperors of Rome but also given the title of *pontifex maximus*, **high priest of the world.**

Through studying history's time line of satanic cult worship, we can see Satan's one-world religion rising out of the revived Roman Empire. Paul warned the New Testament church in 2 Timothy 3:1–7, Peter warned the church in 2 Peter 2:1, and John warned the church in Revelation 3:15–17. This warning stands as firm today for the **terminal generation; it must** not be deceived by Satan's lies.

Revelation 18: Commercial Babylon

Revelation 18 is a difficult chapter in this study in that it requires us to look to the Old Testament for clarity. The Bible is clear that Babylon will be rebuilt, and Babylon is under reconstruction today. This city, however, will fall during the **day of the Lord, in our generation!**

This chapter of Revelation raises questions. Will commercial Babylon be rebuilt as the economic center of the world? Where will Babylon be?

Will Babylon literally be a city or only a symbol of the world political and economic system?

Babylon is a literal city that will outshine all other cities during the tribulation and doubtless serve as the headquarters for the anti-Christ during the first three and a half years of the tribulation. Based on Scripture, it is reasonable to understand that Babylon will be rebuilt; it is currently under a massive construction project on the Euphrates River in Iraq as it was in the prophet Daniel's time for the following reasons.

1. Ancient Babylon was never suddenly and completely destroyed as prophesied in Isaiah 13:19. Babylon fell to the Persians but not according to the end of day's prophecy.
2. The description of Babylon in Jeremiah 51 is very similar to the description given by John in Revelation 18.
3. Babylon is said to be destroyed during the **day of the Lord,** which is the Old Testament term used for the tribulation period or the time of Jacob's trouble (Isaiah 13:6).
4. According to Isaiah 14, Israel will enter into God's rest after Babylon has been destroyed. Israel has not experienced peace or rest for the past 2,000 years following their rejection of the Messiah.
5. Jeremiah predicted that Babylon would drink God's cup of wrath last among the kingdoms of the earth.
6. The vision of the woman in the *ephah* from the prophetic vision of Zechariah 5:5–11 indicates a return to wickedness and commerce in Babylon.
7. The description of Babylon in Revelation 18 is best taken literally.[8]

Theologians and historians have four ideas about Babylon's location, but *only one has a firm scriptural foundation.*

1. The first view puts Babylon in the land of the Chaldeans, where Abraham was called in the covenant promise of God (Genesis

---

8   This list was taken from Scripture and the commentary notes from R. Ludwigson, *Bible Prophecy Notes.*

12:1–3). The land of the Chaldeans is also called the **land of Shinar** (Daniel 1:2), the **land lady of the kingdoms** (Isaiah 47:5), and it is on the Euphrates and Tigris Rivers of **Mesopotamia,** the cradle of civilization and the location of the garden of Eden. Isaiah 14:1–32 suggests Babylon will be in Iraq, in or near modern-day Bagdad.[9] The United States and the European nations are largely funding this project and a vast fiber optic global communications system known as **FLAG. It** is being connected to the world's largest and most expensive U.S. embassy in Bagdad at this time.

2.   The second theory is that Babylon will be Iran, Persia, which will conquer Saudi Arabia and reconstruct Babylon at Mecca during the onset of the tribulation. Isaiah 21:2, 11, 13, and 16 tell us that Iran, **Elam,** will conquer Saudi Arabia. But the location of Mecca for Babylon is doubtful since Mecca is the location of worldwide Muslim worship and the sacred center of Islam.

3.   The third view is the region of the Ur of the Chaldees; **the land of the Chaldea,** which is centered on the Persian Gulf and the current massive building site of Dubai, which currently has the world's tallest structure. Dubai certainly is a good typology of Babylon but does not fit Bible prophecy for the location of Babylon.

4.   The fourth view is that Babylon will be in Iran, **Elam.** But this also is a poor fit with Bible prophecy and Scripture exegesis. Iran is viewed prophetically as a nation that will align with the anti-Christ and the armies of the world in their march on Israel in the last days of the tribulation (Revelation 18:1–8).

Verse 1 opens with a familiar phrase, *meta tauta,* "a change of scene" or "after this" in Greek. This gives us an accurate interpretation and time in Scripture. Commercial Babylon will not suffer destruction until religious Babylon does, and this will be the last form of the Gentile world powers.

Verse 2 is written in the *prophetic aorist tense in Greek* and translates as, "this has never happened before." It has not happened yet, but God views the destruction of commercial Babylon as accomplished, and God's Words

---

9   There are several good websites on the subject of Babylon, including *rebuildingbabylon2012.*

are true. This is significant because Scripture is clear that Babylon will be destroyed and never be rebuilt following the **day of the wrath of God.**

In verse 3, we learn that Babylon, not Wall Street, will become the world's financial center. The United States and the majority of the northern hemisphere is not presented as leading world powers during the tribulation era. (There is one vague if not obscure passage, Ezekiel 38:13, which refers to the North American colonies of once powerful England as "her lion cubs.")

In verses 4 and 5, God tells saints, backsliders, and sinners, "Come out of Babylon." How many times have we listened to warnings for Americans to get out of this or that nation due to civil unrest or war? God has been calling people to safety and salvation since the beginning of Creation; God called Noah and his family out before the flood; He called Abraham out of the Ur of the Chaldees, and He called Lot out of Sodom. God calls the church out before the tribulation in the rapture. If we heed God's call, we will find safety in Jesus Christ. If not, we will perish as Lot's wife did.

In verse 6, we read that God said He would give Babylon a double dose of punishment for her sins (Exodus 22:4, 7, 9 gives the law for the punishment of a thief, a double dose).

Verses 7 and 8 amplify verse 6; Babylon glorified herself as the **queen of the earth.** Isaiah 47:1–8 contains this prophetic phrase, and her destruction is completed in **one day.** Revelation 16:17–19 foretells this, and it will be a literal twenty-four-hour day.

This scene almost appears at atomic and nuclear warfare, swiftly with fire and a cloud, and for the description given by the human view in verses 9 through 19. Atomic, biological, and chemical warfare are certainly possibilities during the tribulation era, but we must remember that our weapons of mass destruction pale in comparison to the power and wrath of God, who can rain fire and brimstone from heaven upon cities; consider Sodom and Gomorrah in Genesis 18.

Revelation 18:9–19: The Human View of Babylon's Destruction

Verses 9 through 11 remind us of the broadcasts we saw of the terrorist attacks on the World Trade Center. The towers fell in one day, the stock market crashed in 1929 in one day, and the prophecy is that Babylon and the global economy will collapse in one day. Scripture captures the human view of this prophetic destruction; the wealthy of the earth mourn for their financial losses, stock prices plummet, and merchandise is consumed by fire in one day. The time to react against this terrible day is now!

In Revelation 11, we read of those who gloried over the death of the **two witnesses, Elijah and Moses. They** gloried over the destruction of religious Babylon, but then they mourned for the judgment of God on their temporal wealth. Matthew 7:1–7 is a fitting epitaph for the masses of Revelation 18: "Judge not lest ye be judged, by what standard ye judge another, you also shall be judged."

The Merchandise of Babylon

Verses 12 through 19 contain the description of commercial Babylon; it reads much like advertisements for Wal-Mart or one of the big-box retail outlet stores. Every imaginable good will be available in Babylon, which will become the world tourist destination, much like the millions in America who visit the Simon Mall in Minneapolis.

Twenty-five of the world's luxuries will be available in Babylon: gold, silver, precious stones and pearls in the jewelry department; fine linen, purple, silk, and scarlet, the colors of the wealthy ruling class in the clothing department; precious wood, ivory, brass, iron, and marble in the home décor department; and building materials in the lumber department. The gourmet department will be filled with spices, cinnamon, and fine foods; in the bath and beauty department, we will see perfume, ointments, and frankincense. In the liquor department will be wine and other forms of alcohol; the deli will boast of oils, fine flours, breads, and sweetcakes; the meat department will have every kind of flesh—beef, mutton, fish; and the pet supply department will have horses and chariots; and then …

The Depravity of Babylon

Gross materialism in Babylon will include human trafficking, the open sale of boys and girls, men and women for prostitution, "the fruits that thy soul lusted after" (v. 14). Only Christ can deliver a man or woman from such depravity. John Newton, who wrote the words to the great Christian hymn, "Amazing Grace," was a slave trader until he received Jesus Christ as Lord and Savior. He called himself the chief of sinners, but upon his repentance, he turned his life to follow Christ and became a preacher of the gospel that "saved a wretch like me."

The fall of Babylon will happen in one hour—sixty minutes. The power of God will consume that great city in swift judgment. In Jesus Christ's parable of the rich fool (Luke 12:16–21) He spoke of a man who planned on living forever on his great wealth; God called him a fool. "Tonight thy soul shall be required of thee and then who shall all these things belong to?" We all are one breath away from eternity; no one has the promise of tomorrow, but we have God's promise that today is the day of salvation if we repent and receive Jesus Christ as our Savior.

I've never read an obituary that read, "He died tomorrow." You might have tied your shoes this morning, but the undertaker might untie them tonight. I have officiated at many funerals, and there are always two unasked questions the mourners have: How much money did he leave behind? Where is he now? The answer to the first question is simple—he or she left it all behind; no Brinks trucks followed the hearse to the cemetery. The second answer depends on the individual's decision in life to accept or to reject Jesus Christ as Savior. If the deceased accepted Christ, he or she is more alive than ever and in the presence of God, Jesus Christ, and the holy angels in heaven. The deceased who rejected Christ is suffering the eternal torments of hell. How will you choose?

Revelation 18:20–24 gives us the angelic view of Babylon. Verse 20 answers the question of the martyrs in heaven to Jesus Christ in Revelation 6:10: "How much longer, Lord?" Jesus replied, "Yet a little while." And then the angels told the saints to rejoice. The day of rejoicing in heaven will be in the fall of Babylon and the swift and imminent end of the tribulation.

In verse 21, a mighty angel seen in Revelation 10:1 took up a mighty stone, like a millstone, and tossed it into the sea. This reference to a millstone is often used by the Old Testament prophets who wrote of Babylon's destruction (Jeremiah 51:63–64). Jesus Christ used the illustration of the millstone when speaking of the judgment for those who hurt children physically, emotionally, or spiritually by preventing them from coming to Christ. It raises a question for those who stand before the **great white judgment throne of God,** lost, unrepentant and required to give an answer for their sins of abortion, murder of the innocents, and perversion, sexual molestation, and rape of children. The angel in this passage concluded with the announcement that Babylon had fallen and shall be found no more.

In verses 22 through 24, the angel explained that Babylon would cease to exist—all nightclub entertainment and music will cease, manufacturing would grind to a halt, and there would be no light and no agricultural products. The greatest judgment tragedy of all is there will be no sense of God and no sorceries (Nahum 3:4). Babylon will be desolate.

The Four Alleluias: Revelation Chapter 19

1. The four alleluias—19:1–6
2. The Marriage Feast of the Lamb—19:7–10
3. The second coming of Christ—19:11–16
4. The Battle of Armageddon—19:17–19
5. The doom of the beast, the anti-Christ, the false prophet, and all those who received the mark of the beast and worshipped it—19:20
6. The doom of the kings of the earth—19:21

Revelation 19 relates the swift end to the tribulation, when the saints in heaven will rejoice over the **Marriage Feast of the Lamb.** Jesus Christ will receive His bride, the universal assembly of born-again believers who make up the **church, the called-out ones, the** *ekklesia.* This glorious event will be celebrated by heaven's greatest praise word, *alleluia,* **or hallelujah.** *Alleluia* in not used anywhere else in the New Testament; the Holy Spirit reserved it for this special occasion. In the Old Testament, the word appears twenty-four times in the Psalms. Heaven will celebrate the Lamb's victory over the harlot church when Jesus marries His bride.

In chapter 19, the Second Advent was revealed, and Jesus brought a swift and final end to humanity's rebellion in the Valley of Megiddo at the Battle of Armageddon with the doom of the anti-Christ, the false prophet, all who took the mark of the beast, and the kings of the earth.

The day of Jehovah is called "The Day" and "The Great Day of the Lord" and is the lengthened period beginning with the Lord's Second Advent and ending in the purgation of the heavens and the earth by fire preparatory to the arrival of the **new heaven and the new earth.** The support Scriptures for this significant and magnificent event are Isaiah 67:17–19, 66:22; 2 Peter 3:13; and Revelation 21:1. Here is the biblical time line of these events.

1. The return of the Lord in glory (Matthew 24:29, 30)
2. The destruction of the beast and his host, the kings of the earth and their armies, and the destruction of the false prophet, which reveal the terrible aspect of that day (Revelation 19:11–21)
3. The judgment of the nations (Zechariah 14:1–9; Matthew 24:31–46)
4. The thousand-year reign of Christ, the **kingdom age,** and the first resurrection of the righteous dead (Revelation 20:4–6)
5. The satanic revolt and its end (Revelation 20:7–10)
6. The second resurrection of the unrighteous dead and the final judgment (Revelation 20:11–15)
7. The **day of God;** the earth is purged by fire (2 Peter 3:10–13)

8. The eternal state and the righteous, redeemed, final destination of the **new earth, from Creation** (Genesis 1:1) to its **re-creation** (Revelation 21:1)

The day of the Lord will be preceded by seven signs.

1. The sending of the prophet Elijah (Malachi 4:5–6; Revelation 11:3–6)
2. Cosmic disturbances (Joel 2:1–12; Matthew 24:29; Acts 2:19; Revelation 6:12–17)
3. The insensibility of the professing church (1 Thessalonians 5:1–3)
4. The apostasy of the professing church in the Laodicean church age and our present **terminal generation** (2 Thessalonians 2:3)
5. Thessalonians 2:1–2 the gathering together in the Rapture of the church
6. The manifestation of the **man of sin, the anti-Christ** (2 Thessalonians 2:1–8)
7. The **apocalyptic judgments** (Revelation 6–18)

Verses 1 through 6 mention that the four alleluias of heaven were sounded out in praise and worship preceding the Marriage Feast of the Lamb with His bride, the church. The first alleluia is given by the saints in heaven for salvation, glory, honor, and power to Jesus Christ, which we translate as, **"Alleluia, because Jesus Christ is worthy."**

The second alleluia from the saints in heaven is an alleluia of praise because Jesus Christ is **true** (John 8:32, 36, 14:6), Christ is **righteous** (1 John 3:7), He judged the great whore, religious Babylon, and He avenged the blood of His servants (Romans 12:19), and the smoke of Babylon rose up forever and ever. Amen!

The third alleluia is from the twenty-four elders and the four angelic creatures at the throne of God (Revelation 4:4–11) saying that Christ was the amen (Revelation 3:14), and saying praise God, fear God all ye His servants, both small and great.

The fourth alleluia is from all the saints in heaven; they shout and sing, **"Alleluia, because the Lord God omnipotent reigns!"**

In verses 7 through 10, we read of the **Marriage Feast of the Lamb. T**his intriguing passage gives us great joy and expectation of this celebration, but the Bible leaves much unsaid about the ceremony. This feast is much like our own earthly wedding days; we knew they were special, we knew there would be family and friends gathered, and we knew there would be dinner parties and gifts.

The Jewish wedding is a great example and biblical typology of the Marriage Feast of the Lamb in heaven. In Matthew 1:18–19, we learn that Mary was engaged to Joseph. The Jewish engagement period required the couple to behave as though they were already married. The groom proposed at the bride's home, but they did not consummate the marriage until a year later. At that time, having observed the faithfulness of the couple to live a separated and sanctified life before each other, before family and community, the father of the groom would tell his son to bring his wife home for the feast, celebration, and consummation of the marriage. If one of the parties defiled himself or herself with immorality during the espousal period, a writ of divorce was required.

Jesus Christ came and proposed to us (Galatians 4:4; John 3:16; Revelation 3:20), and as Christians, we accepted Christ's proposal to be saved, pure, and faithful to Him until He returned for us. Jesus Christ is with the Father in heaven, and God will send Him for His bride at the rapture of the church to receive the dead and alive in Christ since the day of Pentecost (John 14:1–6; Revelation 4:1; 1 Thessalonians 4:13–18; 1 Corinthians 15:51–57). At that time, Jesus will bring us to His Father's house in heaven, and our marriage to Jesus Christ will be spiritually consummated at the Marriage Feast of the Lamb.

We must make ourselves ready to be received by King Jesus (Esther 2:9, 12–13). Jesus Christ delivered a great parable on the necessity of preparation and anticipation in Matthew 25:1–13. In that parable of the ten virgins, five were wise, prepared, ready, and waiting, while five were foolish, having never accepted the marriage proposal of Jesus Christ to be saved; they lacked the oil (the Holy Spirit) of assurance that would have sealed their lives unto the Lord by the Holy Spirit of God (Ephesians 1:13–14).

In verse 8, the wife wore a white linen robe, representative of the righteousness of the saints, which requires an original word study that translates as "**righteous deeds**"; the bride's wedding garment was made up of the righteous deeds done by the saints. The bride was righteous because of the righteousness of Christ, and the bride was clothed for her wedding because of her acts of mercy, generosity, grace, and goodness shown to others as the love of Christ. We take note of Revelation 14:13: "The works of the saints follow them."

We are all preparing unique wedding garments in life today. There is nothing more special to a bride than to have a one-of-a-kind wedding dress. We are creating our own; some will be simple, some very ornate, and sadly, some will look like an old, white feed sacks. Those will be worn by some who have never served the Lord or witnessed and shown His grace and mercy to others.

Revelation 19:9 gives us the reason to rejoice: "Blessed are they which are called to the Marriage Supper of the Lamb." You must RSVP if you want to attend this wedding. The Bible instructs, "This is a true saying of God." You must respond to the invitation of Christ in this life to be your Lord and Savior; the plan of salvation calls on us to submit our free will before the Lord and accept His gift of forgiveness of sins and salvation.

The marriage supper will be unlike any meal you have ever attended. The angels will be serving, the angelic choir will be singing, the harpers will be playing, and we will sit with Jesus. The feast will last according to some theologians for one year; other theologians figure on seven years. The best fit from Scripture is one month, between the fall of commercial Babylon and Christ's Second Advent. The rationale for this is in the very specific alleluia praises of the saints in heaven, the necessity of the harlot church's fall, and the wording of chapter 19, with the bride arrayed in fine white linen. In chapter 20, with the Second Advent of Christ, we see the saints in fine white linen riding back with Jesus Christ, ending the great tribulation.

There is a brief intermission in the Scriptures here when John was so overwhelmed by the sights of the marriage feast, so full of the Spirit of praise, worship, and adoration that when one of the elders approached him, he fell down and worshipped the elder (Revelation 19:10). The elder told John to worship God, for the testimony of Jesus is the Spirit of prophecy. This is very important; prophecy came by the Word, and Jesus Christ is the Word (John 1:1); all Scripture is given by the inspiration of God (2 Timothy 3:16).

Verses 11 through 16 reveal Christ's Second Advent. **At His First Advent, He was** born of the seed of a woman (Genesis 3:15); He was born of a virgin (Isaiah 7:14); He was born in Bethlehem (Micah 5:2); He was born in the fullness of time (Galatians 4:4); He was born without a sin nature (2 Corinthians 5:21); and His arrival was according to promises of God throughout the Old Testament.

Angels announced Christ's birth; Joseph and Mary held Him, and the shepherds worshipped Him. The magi followed His star and presented Him with gifts and worship. He was born a King in a manger, the Lamb of God, and Satan tried to have Him killed through the jealousy of Herod the Great.

Joseph, Mary, and Jesus fled to Egypt upon the instruction of the angel and fulfilled prophecy: "My Son have I called out of Egypt." Jesus grew up in Nazareth and was called a Nazarene according to prophecy. After His death, burial, and resurrection, He ascended to glory at the right hand of the Father, where He intercedes for us.

It has now been 2,000 years since Christ's ascension; the next great cataclysmic world event for our present **terminal generation will be the rapture of the church. It** will occur suddenly, soon, and secretly from the world's view and will be a uniquely Christian experience. Jesus said, "Behold I come quickly." Revelation 4:1, 2 Thessalonians 2:1–2, 1 Thessalonians 4:13–18, and 1 Corinthians 15:51–57 give details and the order of events of the rapture. It is solely a New Testament Christian experience, so be prepared!

Christ's **Second Advent** is revealed in 19:11–16. John recorded for us the order of the events in the return of Christ.

1. A door will be opened in heaven, the advent door. This door was opened only one time before; this time, it will be seen and witnessed by all.
2. A white horse will transport the King of Kings. When Christ entered Jerusalem on Palm Sunday, He did so publicly and prophetically on the exact date as revealed in Daniel's vision of the seventy weeks of years, humbly riding a colt that had never before been ridden. Upon Christ's Second Advent, He will return as the warrior King.
3. There is one name of the Christ that is above all other names—Jesus, the only begotten Son of God with us (Isaiah 7:14; John 1:14). There are thirty-six names ascribed to Jesus Christ in the New Testament, but at the name of Jesus, every knee shall bow, and every tongue will confess that He is the Son of the Living God. From the description John gave us in verses 11–13, we see a glimpse of His glory; Christ is the faithful and true and is called the Word of God.
4. Jesus will be wearing the crown of a king (actually, it translates as "many crowns" or "diadems").
5. The armies of heaven, the saints, will follow Him.
6. He will be clothed in a vesture dipped in the blood of the martyrs.
7. The Word of God will proceed out of His mouth, and it will be called the sword of the Spirit (Ephesians 6:17).
8. Jesus Christ will smite all the nations that have gathered in battle against Israel in the Valley of Megiddo.
9. Jesus Christ will have written on His vesture "King of Kings" and "Lord of Lords."

Verses 17 through 19 deal with the Battle of Armageddon. There are several theological views of this battle; the proper biblical interpretation is to not confuse the numerous historical battles that have been fought throughout the ages in the Megiddo Valley. The Battle of Armageddon in Revelation 19 was led by the anti-Christ against the Lamb of God and against God's people and nation of Israel. The battle was fought and won by Christ in one hour. The battle was described in Daniel 11:40–45, Joel 3:9–17, Zechariah 14:1–3, and Revelation 16:14–16. It occurred in the final days of the great tribulation; John wrote that the kings of the earth would gather "for the war of the Great Day of God, the Almighty, in a place known as **Harmagedon**" (Revelation 16:14–16).

Several battles will occur at this time, and great armies will assemble in the Valley of Esdraelon in northern Israel. According to the Bible, armies from the East and West will gather on this plain, and the anti-Christ will defeat the armies of the South who will threaten his power. He will destroy revived Babylon in the East before turning his forces toward Jerusalem to destroy it. As the anti-Christ's army moves toward Jerusalem, God will intervene, and Jesus Christ will return and rescue His people. The Lord and His angelic host will destroy the armies, capture the anti-Christ and the false prophet, and cast them into hell (Revelation 19:11–12). When the Lord returns, the power and the rule of the anti-Christ will end.

This battle is often referred to as the final revolt of evil against God by His enemy and our adversary, Satan. This is an incorrect inference and speculation. There is yet one more battle; it will occur at the end of Christ's thousand-year reign. In many ways, that final battle will surpass Armageddon. The final revolt of evil was recorded in Revelation 20:7–9 and Ezekiel 38–39; it is referred to correctly as Ezekiel's war. This final revolt of evil will be led by Satan; it will be spearheaded by Russia; armies and nations will gather against Israel for its wealth with which it will have been blessed by God during Christ's millennial reign. **Gog** is called the **Prince of Rosh; Magog** is where **Gog** is worshipped. **Rosh** is **Russia,** the land to the far north, Siberia. Its major cities are **Mesheck,** which translates as Moscow, and **Tubal,** which translates as **Tubolsh.** The prophet Ezekiel listed the five nations from the north that will come down to wage war on Israel (Ezekiel 38:1–11): **Persia** (Iran), **Ethiopia** (southern Africa), **Libya (northern Africa), Togarmah (southern Russia)**, and this will include a host of armies that will join and fight alongside the Russian invasion, including those from **Gomar** (Germany), and the armies of the East, **the orient, China, and India**.

Verse 20 of Revelation 19 reveals the doom and destination of the **beast of the sea**, the anti-Christ, the **beast of the earth**, the false prophet, all who received the **mark of the beast,** and those who worshipped his image. They will be cast into hell.

In verse 21, we learn the doom of the kings of the earth, and this is parenthetical to verses 17–19. Although these kings were slain, they will not receive the final judgment until the second resurrection of the unrighteous dead, and then they will stand before God at the great white throne.

The Thousand-Year Reign of Christ: Revelation 20

1. Satan bound for a thousand years—20:1–3
2. The first resurrection of the righteous dead—20:4–6
3. Satan loosed, the doom of Gog and Magog—20:7–9
4. Satan doomed—20:10
5. The doom of unbelievers, the second resurrection of the unrighteous dead, the great white throne of God, the lake of fire, and the second death—20:11–15

God has given us many specific times throughout Scripture to make Bible prophecy clear and concise. The Old Testament foretold the First Advent of Jesus Christ, the New Testament was the unveiling of His life and His Second Advent. God's prophetic clock in Scripture sounds out a warning to our present generation: "Prepare to meet thy God."

In God's message to the prophets of the Old Testament who predicted the birth of Jesus, Mary was identified, the family lineage and genealogy of Jesus Christ was identified, the location of Christ's birth was identified, and the exact date and day of Jesus' entrance into Jerusalem for His passion was identified (Isaiah 7:14, 9:6–7, 53:1–6; Daniel 9:24–27; Micah 5:2). Every one of these prophecies given centuries before the First Advent was fulfilled exactly according to Scripture. Jesus' resurrection was identified as being on the third day following His crucifixion (John 2:19). The gift of the Holy Spirit sent from God was given as exactly fifty days following Christ's resurrection at the day of Pentecost or Feast of Pentecost (Leviticus 23:15–16).

Scripture does not give the date of the rapture of the church. Jesus said that only the Father knew; this carries us back to Revelation 19 and the illustration of the Hebrew wedding. Jesus said the rapture of the church would be preceded by signs, insensitivity in the church, apostasy in the church, and a falling away from the church (2 Thessalonians 2:2–4). In His Olivet Discourse, Jesus said the rapture would occur after a long period following His ascension (Matthew 25:14–19). Jesus promised to return for His bride (John 14:3), and we are informed where we will meet the Lord—in the air (1 Thessalonians 4:13–18; 1 Corinthians 15:51–57). Jesus did not give the apostles or the disciples the exact date, but He exhorted all believers to watch and wait in earnest expectation of His sudden and soon return every day. Two thousand years have passed, and Christ's return for His church is closer than it has ever been; this present age of grace is drawing quickly to a close for this terminal generation.

The time and order of the events that we do know from Scripture and the revealed prophetic words of Revelation establish a great sense of urgency for our generation to read, to hear, and to obey these prophecies or be left behind for the terror of the great tribulation. Here is God's prophetic clock of end-time events.

1. The seven years of the Tribulation will last exactly 2,520 days according to the Jewish calendar and will begin following the rapture of the church with the revealing of the anti-Christ, the man of sin, the son of perdition.

2. The seven years of the tribulation will cease with Christ's victorious Second Advent with His saints and angels from glory. At that time, the beast of the sea, the anti-Christ, the beast of the earth, the false prophet, and all who received the mark of the beast will be cast alive into the lake of fire.

3. Christ's millennial reign will begin seventy-five days later, according to Daniel 12:11–13; this accounts for the additional seventy-five days added to the 2,520 days of the tribulation and great tribulation. This time is for the purification of the tribulation temple and the priest and the judgment of the nations as declared by Jesus Christ in Matthew 25:31–46. This time will also accomplish the cleaning and the clearing of the debris from the Battle of Armageddon, the smiting stone of Daniel 2:34–35.

4. The kingdom of Christ will last 1,000 years (Revelation 20:1–6). The theocratic rule of God through Jesus Christ, the King of Kings and Lord of Lords, will be established with David serving as coregent (2 Samuel 7:4–17), and the Davidic covenant will be fulfilled. Zerubbabel will serve as the signet prime minister (Haggai 2:23).

5. After the 1,000 years, Satan will be loosed for a season, the armies of the North and world nations, Gog, and Magog, will descend upon Israel for the wealth of the nation (Ezekiel 38–39). They will be defeated by God, and Satan will be judged and condemned to the lake of fire. God will hold court for the unrighteous dead at His great white throne, and then eternity begins; there will be time no more (Revelation 21:22).

Time is calculated in Bible prophecy according to the Jewish calendar of 360 days in a year. The most extensive example of biblical prophetic time is in the short book of Haggai, which contains only thirty-eight verses, but it gives the exact year, month, and day. Additionally, the Jewish day is divided into two equal twelve-hour portions, 6:00 a.m. to 6 p.m. is the day, and 6:00 p.m. to 6:00 a.m. is the night. Any portion of a Jewish day is counted as a full day. God established time, days, weeks, months, and years for humans to order their lives. All creation was established on a lunar cycle, not a solar cycle: "The evening and the morning were the first day" (Genesis 1:5).

This cycle of life is witnessed in the female fertility cycle, the tides of the oceans, and the seas, which are on a lunar cycle, and spring, summer, fall, and winter are all according to the lunar cycle from full moon to full moon.

In verses 1 through 3, Michael the Archangel came down from heaven (Revelation 12:7) and chained Satan in the bottomless pit, the abyss (*Hades* in Greek, *sheol* in Hebrew, and *tartaros* in Greek). Satan was restrained in the bottomless pit for a thousand years. During this time, the kingdom of Christ on earth benefitted from a perfect and righteous theocratic rule in fulfillment of the prophecy of Isaiah 9:6–7.

In Revelation 20:1–3, we learn that Satan was not captive in the abyss of hell because of the location but because the seal of the Living God was upon his dungeon door, and that seal could not be broken or crossed. The seal of the Living God on the Christian soul also cannot be broken (Ephesians 1:13–14; Romans 8:38–39).

In verses 4 through 6, we read of the first resurrection of the righteous dead, which will include all the Old Testament saints' bodies and all the tribulation saints' bodies. Paul instructed in his epistle about the immediacy of the righteous souls' return to the Lord at the very moment of death: "Absent from the body is to be present with the Lord." Solomon wrote, "The soul returns to God who gave it" (Ecclesiastes 12:7). We must not confuse the rapture of the church with the first or second resurrection. The rapture of the church is uniquely a Christian event; the Word of God states, "The dead in Christ shall rise first at the trumpet call and then those of us which are alive and remain will be caught up in the air to be with the Lord forever." The bodies of the Old Testament righteous dead will not be raised until the first resurrection; however, their captive souls in paradise were set free and delivered to heaven following Christ's atonement sacrifice on the cross (1 John 2:2; Colossians 2:13–14). These resurrected Old Testament saints will rule and reign with Jesus Christ for a thousand years (Ezekiel 37) and his vision of the Valley of Dry Bones, resurrected to life as the restored nation and remnant of Israel.

The unrighteous dead will comprise all unrepentant sinners' bodies since Creation; they will not be resurrected until the great white judgment throne of God. The souls of the unrighteous dead are in Hades, suffering the torments and the terrors of rejecting Jesus Christ (Luke 16:19–31).

Verses 7 through 9 tell us that when the thousand-year reign of Christ concludes, Satan will be loosed to deceive the nations again. The nations of the earth will be repopulated by those who did not perish in the tribulation, and Israel will be repopulated by the remnant preserved by God. The millennial reign of Christ will establish a unique environment on earth. Satan will be bound, and perfect peace, rule, and justice will be established on earth. Israel will receive the promised inheritance of the land, and the nations of the earth will pour into Israel to praise and worship Jesus Christ. (A great study of the millennium and the future restoration of Israel as promised by God in the Old Testament is in Isaiah 54:1–55:13.) The primary subject of the millennium is Jesus Christ's rule and reign but also His relationship with Israel.

1. Israel will be reaccepted by God as foretold by Hosea and Isaiah (39–66).
2. Israel will grow during the millennium (Isaiah 54:1–3).
3. Israel's reproach will be taken away (Isaiah 54:4–6).
4. Israel's future salvation will be like the Noahic Covenant (Isaiah 54:9–10).
5. The inhabitants of restored Israel (Isaiah 54:13–14).
6. Israel will be restored (Isaiah 55:12–13).
7. Israel will be in its glory (Isaiah 56:1–58:12).
8. Israel will reflect the light of the world (Isaiah 60:1–4).

In verse 10, we learn that Satan, after his last rebellion, will be cast into the lake of fire, where he will be tormented. Many have asked, "If God had Satan bound and humanity was free from the presence of temptation and sin, why did God let Satan out for a little while?" This is because in the garden of Eden, there was absolute perfection, a perfect environment, and a perfect food supply. Man and woman were created in perfection in the image of God; they had a perfect, harmonious relationship with God and a perfect family relationship with each other. God said, "It is good!"

Sin entered the human race when Adam and Eve sinned; this corrupted creation. God created Adam and Eve for relationship and fellowship. God did not create mindless robots; He created humanity, His highest order of creation, to love, honor, obey, and to fellowship with Him by a free-will decision to love, serve, and obey Him.

During the millennial reign of Christ, the world will once again be a theocracy, and all will revert to perfection because of the absence of temptation and sin in the world with the binding of Satan.

At Creation and during the millennial reign of Christ, people will have free will, and God's holiness requires our free-will choice to love, obey, serve, and honor Him.

The loosing of Satan validates the righteous judgment of God upon sin and the just rewards for the obedient saint. This is a constant reminder to the human race that apart from Christ, humanity will do only evil. God's grace removes the curse of temptation and sin and the presence of sin from this world once and for all.

Verses 11 through 15 cover the second resurrection of the unrighteous dead who will stand before the throne of God to be judged out of the books. The late, great evangelist and preacher D. L. Moody said, "To be born once is to die twice, but to be born twice is to die but once." D. L. Moody had this passage of Scripture in mind with that quote. Simply put, you must be born again (John 3:1–17).

The books that will be opened for the judgment of the unrighteous dead are found in the Old and the New Testaments.

1. The Book of the Generations—this identifies a person as being a part of the human race as created by God in the garden and under His authority.
2. The Book of the Law—the Commandments, the ordinances, and the statutes of God as sovereign Judge of humanity.
3. The Book of the Works—the works of humans from birth to death.

4. The Lamb's Book of Life—the names of all who have received Jesus Christ as their Lord and Savior and stand guiltless and free from the wrath of God (Romans 5:1, 8:1; John 3:16, 17; 1 John 5:12–13).

Sadly, in the American justice system are men and women incarcerated who are innocent; the news carries the stories of those vindicated and set free due to advances in forensic techniques and DNA analysis or from new evidence arising that vacated their convictions. Although the numbers of the innocent are small compared to the numbers of the guilty, one innocent person behind bars is too many!

No innocent people, however, will be present before God at His throne of judgment, standing to give accounts for their great sin of rejecting Jesus Christ and God's gift of salvation. Not one righteous saved saint will stand in judgment to hell, and this is the omniscience of God at work; He knows all things as the perfect and holy Judge of sin, transgressions, and the iniquities of the transgressor. All at this throne will be judged guilty as charged!

There are three primary doctrinal views of eschatology or end-times prophetic events: amillennialism, postmillennialism, and premillennialism. Only premillennialism passes the test of the plenary interpretation of Bible prophecy as literal. The truth of the millennial reign of Christ cannot be dismissed as being only symbolic or allegorical or be spiritualized away. To remove the millennial reign of Christ from the Bible would require its disembowelment. Clearly, 28 percent of the Bible is prophetic; it reveals God's plan for the ages from eternity past to eternity future, and His nation of Israel is a primary theme.

Why must there be a millennial reign of Christ?

1. To fulfill the covenant promises that God gave Abraham, Moses, David, Joshua, Daniel, Jeremiah, Isaiah, and Ezekiel in the Mosaic, Abrahamic, Palestinian, and the Davidic Covenants.
2. To fulfill the Father's promise to His Son that the kingdoms of the world would be His to reign over.

3. To fulfill the veracity of God's recorded Word (Titus 1:2: God cannot lie) in that Bible prophecy must be fulfilled 100 percent in accordance with the inspired Word of God, and this encompasses every prophetic word spoken to the prophets of old.[10]

The Seven New Things: Revelation 21:1–22:7

1. The new heaven and the new earth—21:1–2
2. The new people—21:3–8
3. The new Jerusalem—21:9–21
4. The new temple—21:22
5. The new light—21:23–27
6. The new paradise and the river of life—22:1–7

In Revelation 21:5, Jesus Christ declared, "Behold, I make all things new." This statement carries us back to the earliest chapters of Genesis in which we learn about God's creative power. The word *creation* and the very *act of creation* by the spoken words of God demand a moment of meditation and study. The scientific world and evolutionists today are perplexed and left without an argument of reason or explanation for three great questions concerning the d*octrine of Creation*.

1. What was the source of the elements that make up the universe? Where did the cosmic gases, atomic elements, and proteins originate since the characteristic of self-existence may be ascribed only to a sovereign creator?
2. The *evolutionary theory for the origin of humanity* cannot answer the complexity of the design of human anatomy and physiology and the mental, emotional, and spiritual nature in the design of humans much less the inferior creatures of creation. The genetic code and the complexity of human DNA reveal the reality of Creation by design. Human sexuality demands that both must have been

---

10   There are several great commentaries on the study of prophecy and eschatology available today, including Wayne Grudem, *Systematic Theology*; LaHaye and Hindson, *The Popular Encyclopedia of Bible Prophecy*; and Carson and Moo, *Introduction to the New Testament*.

created in the same generation and not during eons of evolutionary time. Any gap of one generation would have doomed humanity to extinction due to the lack of ability to procreate. Humans did not climb out of a primal cesspool or from the evolutionary incubator of time to become the highest order by chance.

3. What existed before the universes if not God?

The only reasonable and logical conclusion will not be found in science but in the eyewitness testimony of the Creator of all things, God. The perfect, detailed, inerrant, and infallible words of Bible prophecy validate the Bible, from Genesis to Revelation, as inspired, acceptable, and true. Prophecy as recorded in the Word of God stands as final authentication of God's self-existence, omniscience, omnipotence, omnipresence, and eternality.

Genesis 1:1 tells us, "In the beginning, God created ..." In a brief word study of Creation from the original languages of the Bible, we look to the word choice of "create," or *bara'*, which means "to make from nothing." This alone answers the question of what existed in the universe before Creation—nothing but the self-existence of a triune God.

Second, we look to the creative power of God; the word is *exousia,* which refers to the ability to create. God displayed His **exousia power** in His act of Creation by the spoken word (Genesis 1:3): "God said, let there be light, and there was light." This initial act of Creation is the answer to the question posed by skeptics, evolutionists, and atheists, "What was the first act, the initiator of it all?" The first act was the Word of God. This act of Creation by God was displayed as His *dunamis,* His miraculous power. The Greek word *logos* translates as the Word of God in an **expression of thought and action!**

In the beginning, God created the heavens and the earth, and the Trinity is revealed in the first chapters of Genesis. The Godhead is seen in Genesis 1:1, the Holy Spirit is revealed in Genesis 1:2, and the Son of God is revealed in the image of God given to humanity foreshadowing the coming incarnation of Son in the image of the Father (John 1:14; Philippians 2:5–8). The great testimony of God and the first **Trinitarian formula in**

the Bible is in Genesis 1:26–27, when God said, "Let us make man in our own image."

At Creation, eternity past met time, when all things in God's creative week were made by them. God the Father owned "the earth and the fullness thereof" (Psalm 50:12). Jesus Christ was the architect; "For by him all things were created, that are in heaven and that are in the earth, and he is before all things, and by him all things consist" (Colossians 1:15–19; John 14:3). The Holy Spirit was the labor force, the power of God in Creation and the preserving power of creation (Genesis 1:2).

It was therefore entirely appropriate for Jesus Christ to declare, "Behold, I make all things new." This authority was given to the Son by the Father as recorded in Ephesians 3:9: "the mystery of God, who created all things by Jesus Christ." In the study of Revelation 21, we will see seven things made new.

In verses 1 and 2, John saw the glorious and grand vision of the new heaven and the new earth as the prophecies of the Old Testament prophets and the New Testament words of Jesus Christ were fulfilled.

The first heaven, our atmosphere, and the old earth will be purified by fire. Satan and unrepentant sinners will have been judged to the lake of fire, and humanity will prepare to step into the pristine perfection of re-creation (2 Peter 3:10–11; Revelation 20:10–15).

John saw new Jerusalem coming down from God in heaven. This new city was described as a stationary city floating above the earth in space like a giant satellite encircling the starry capital from which the earth will receive light (Revelation 21:24–25).

And there will be no more sea. We must not confuse the millennial nature of the earth with the eternal nature of the new heaven and the new earth. In the millennium, there will be oceans, seas, rivers, and lakes, and even the Dead Sea will be alive again from the purifying waters that flow down the steps of the millennial temple in Jerusalem (Ezekiel 47:1–12).

In verses 3 through 8, John heard a voice out of heaven, the third heaven, God's abode. The tabernacle of God was with men. God will dwell with people again as He did with Adam and Eve (Genesis 3:8) and Enoch (Genesis 5:24). Because sin was cancelled, the curse of sin was removed, and the presence of Satan had been taken away forever, God once again had fellowship with His highest order of creation, humanity. The great separation of humanity from all other created things is fourfold.

1. We were created in the image of the Living God (Genesis 1:26).
2. We were given souls and the spirit of life (Genesis 2:7).
3. We were all given a measure of faith at Creation to believe in God as seen through the essence of all created things (Psalm 19:1–6; Romans 12:3).
4. We were reconciled with God by the atoning sacrifice of Jesus Christ on the cross (1 John 2:2; Colossians 2:13–14; 2 Corinthians 5:21; Romans 5:1; Romans 8:1), and we were sealed by the Holy Spirit of God until the day of Redemption (Ephesians 1:13–14), and therefore we are secure in the Father's hand (Romans 8:38–39).

In verse 3, we begin to learn the occupants of this new city: God the Father (Revelation 4:2–3, 5:1–7), the Son of God (Revelation 5:6), the Holy Spirit (Revelation 14:13, 22:17), the holy angels and the elect angels (Hebrews 12:22; Revelation 5:11), and these will include the seraphim (Isaiah 6:1–7), the cherubim (Psalm 80:1, 99:1, Revelation 4:6–8), Gabriel (Daniel 8:6, 9:21; Luke 1:11,19), and the Archangel Michael (Daniel 10:13, 21, 12:1; Jude 1:9; Revelation 12:7), the twenty-four elders around the throne (Revelation 4:4), the saved saint of Israel (Hebrews 11:16; Matthew 25:10, 23; Revelation 14:1–3, 15:1–3). The church, the bride of Christ, comprises all born-again believers in the gospel (Hebrews 12:22–23; Revelation 19:1, 7–8, 21:9–11) and all the redeemed, repentant sinners since Creation (Revelation 5:9, 7:9–11).

This raises the question, who won't be in heaven? The answer is given in Revelation 21:8, the fearful (those who do not have the sealing saving Spirit of God in their lives), the unbelieving (those who have never accepted Jesus Christ as their Lord and Savior and have not repented and confessed their sins and embraced by faith the death, burial, and resurrection of Jesus Christ). This group of poor, lost souls will be identified by their abominable nature, character, and actions; they will be the whoremongers, sorcerers, idolaters, and liars.

God will wipe away all tears in heaven. It is important to note that there are tears in heaven; the martyrs wept and cried out to Jesus in Revelation 6:10, and the tears God wiped away in Revelation 21:4 reveal that the saints in heaven have tears, but the context makes them tears of sorrow and pain. This passage does not indicate we will not have tears of rejoicing. Tears and the emotion of joy are part of our human nature. Our tears will be wiped away because there is no more death (Romans 6:23) because the curse of sin will be gone (Genesis 3:14–19).

Jesus Christ will make all things new, not reinvented but renewed to the original condition—pristine and perfect. It is important to remember that the garden of Eden was a specific location; it did not cover the earth, but the goodness of God's creation did. We will experience the glory of the earth as God intended for us to enjoy.

Verses 9 through 21 deal with the Lamb's bride and the new Jerusalem. In beginning of Revelation 21, John described the beauty of the new Jerusalem as a bride who was holy, chaste, pure, and lovely and who had been prepared for Jesus Christ. Just as He is preparing a place for us in glory and on the earth to rule and to reign with Him for eternity as stated in John 14:3, God the Father is also preparing new Jerusalem.

New Jerusalem (Revelation 21:26) measures 1,500 miles long, wide, and high. The new Jerusalem would reach from New York to Denver and from Canada to Florida.

The shape of new Jerusalem is a perfect cube. We populate earth's surface, but in the new Jerusalem, the heavenly inhabitants populate the inside, possibly much like Noah and his family lived in the ark. The walls of the city are 216 feet high (Revelation 21:12, 17–18) and are made of jasper, a crystal-clear diamond.

The gates of heaven total twelve, just like Old Jerusalem. Each gate is guarded by angel gatekeepers, greeters, and guides, much like church greeters direct people into the sanctuary to meet God. The gates are each carved out of a giant pearl, and on each gate is inscribed the name of one of the individual tribes of Israel, the twelve sons of Jacob. Note that the pearl is the important point of the text because it is the one jewel that denotes the church. Just like the irritating grain of sand that forms the pearl, we wounded Christ, we were ugly in sin, but Christ covered us with righteousness. The beauty was not the grain of sand, but God sees us as lovely in Christ, a pearl of great price as described in Matthew 13:45–46.

The foundations of heaven are twelve layers of stone, each a different precious jewel. Each layer contains the names of the twelve apostles (Revelation 21:14, 19–20).

The streets of heaven are made of pure, transparent gold, as are the houses. The throne will be there for all to see and to worship the Lord, who is seated on the throne. The River of Life will flow throughout heaven (Revelation 22:1), and The Tree of Life (Revelation 22:2) that was taken from the garden of Eden due to humanity's sin is now blossoming and bearing fruit in heaven again.

The worship center will be unlike any we have ever seen or any church we have ever entered. It is grand, it is glorious, and it is an open design, and all are welcome to enter. There are no courts of separation; Jews and Gentiles alike may worship the Lord without separation. There are no denominational worship centers in heaven, only the tabernacle of God for all believers. One can only imagine the sights and sounds that await us.

The light source will be the glory of God (Genesis 1:3). This does not imply there will be no sun, moon, or stars. The Word of God is clear (Revelation 21:23): "The city had no need of the sun, neither the moon to shine." The glory of God lightened it, and the Lamb is the Light.

What will heaven be like for you and me? It will be a place of learning (1 Corinthians 13:9–10), a place of singing (Isaiah 44:23; Hebrews 2:9, 12; Revelation 14:3, 15:3), and a place of service (Revelation 22:3, 7:15; 2

Timothy 2:12). Heaven will be a place of fellowship (1 Corinthians 13:12), and it will not be boring, so don't pack magazines or tablets.

The Last Message in the Bible: Revelation 22:8–21

1. The last message—22:8–15
   a. Keep the Word of God obediently and worship God—22:8–9
   b. Don't seal this book, share it—22:10
   c. The separation of the just from the unjust—22:11
   d. "I come quickly, my reward is with me, I am the Alpha and the Omega, the First and the Last"—22:12–13
   e. Blessed are the obedient, cursed are the outcast—22:14–15
2. The last promise—22:16–20
   a. Hear the word of this prophecy; come to Jesus—22:16–17
   b. Cursed are those who add to or take away from these prophetic words—22:18–19
3. The last prayer of the Bible—22:21

The Revelation of Jesus Christ is the only prophetic book in the New Testament, and the **will of God bleeds across every verse of Scripture** from the introduction to the closing prayer. The thin red line of Revelation is the **shed blood of righteousness** that flowed from the broken body of Jesus Christ, the Lamb of God, sacrificed for our sins 2,000 years ago. God is not willing any should perish, and throughout the Bible, His call to repentance and salvation rings like a bell tolling out the warning, "You must be born again." Much has been written in this study about Israel as God's chosen country and about the Gentile nations. The Jewish and the Gentile nations are the elect of God chosen before the foundations of the world. The gospel of Jesus Christ is available to all who will receive Him and be saved (Romans 1:16), "For I am not ashamed of the gospel of Christ for it is the power of God unto salvation to everyone that believeth, to the Jew first, and also the Greek."

One of the greatest words in all of Scripture is *whosoever!* In John 3:16, we find whosoever receives God's gift of Jesus Christ into their hearts and lives will receive the promise of everlasting life. In Revelation 3:20, we find whosoever opens the door of their hearts and invites Jesus Christ in will receive the presence of Christ into their lives. The urgency of the hour for our terminal **generation** is in the Old and the New Testament, Isaiah 49:8 and 2 Corinthians 6:2, "Today is the accepted time, and today is the Day of Salvation."

God is just and has given equally to all a measure of faith for the capacity to believe in the Son of God. God's will was established in the **incarnation of Jesus** for all humanity (John 1:14). God's provision is in the span of His Son's sacrifice from the tip of His left hand to the tip of Jesus Christ right hand on the cross that reaches out to all humanity (1 John 2:2). God's provision is in His inspired Word available to all (2 Timothy 3:16). God reveals His patience in this provision of time; God has given to all a twenty-four-hours day, no more and no less, and today is the day of salvation.

The great question for our generation is a decision to receive Jesus Christ and be saved or reject Him and be left behind in sins and face the coming darkness of the great tribulation. This will be the difference between gaining salvation or suffering hell, safety or sorrow, peace or punishment, eternal delight or eternal damnation. The choice is one of free will, and it is yours to make—no decision is a decision of regret.

In verses 8 and 9, John, having seen and heard those things contained in the first seven verses of chapter 22, was overwhelmed by the sights and sounds and fell at the feet of the angel who showed him those things. The angel instructed John to not worship him but to obey and worship God. I find interesting the multitude of things humanity will worship. In America, most do not bow to a shrine of wood or stone, but American society in general has embraced idolatry in what it worships, in whom it worships, and in how and when it worships.

The Bible instructs us that God placed the desire in man's heart to worship Him, but due to the sin of Adam and Eve, this desire was corrupted. Romans 1:18–25 tells us,

The wrath of God is revealed from heaven against all ungodliness and unrighteousness of men, who hold the truth in unrighteousness, because that which may be known of God is manifest in them, for God hath showed it unto them. For the invisible things of him from the Creation of the world are clearly seen, being understood by the things that are made, even His Eternal Godhead, so they are without excuse, because that when they knew God, they glorified him not as God, neither were thankful, but became vain in their imaginations and their foolish heart was darkened. Professing themselves to be wise, they became fools [Psalm 14:1]. And changed the glory of the incorruptible God into the image made like to corruptible man, and to birds, and four-footed beast, and creeping things. Wherefore God also gave them up to uncleanness through the lust of their own hearts, to dishonor their own bodies between themselves.

In 2 Timothy 3:1–7, we read,

This know also, that in the last days perilous times shall come. For men shall be lovers of their own selves, covetous, boasters, proud, blasphemers, disobedient to parents, unthankful, unholy. Without natural affection, truce breakers, false accusers, incontinent, fierce, despisers of those that are good. Traitors, heady, high-minded, lovers of pleasure more than lovers of God. Having a form of godliness, but denying the power thereof, from such turn away. For of this sort are they which creep into houses and lead captive silly women laden with sins, led away with diver's lust. Ever learning and never able to come to the knowledge of truth.

Idolatry in America is manifested in the worship of sports and athletic events, which can become the overriding priority of our youth and adults from preschool to professional sports. It is seen in movies, concerts, nightclubs, casinos, and social clubs. Addiction to drugs, alcohol, gambling, immorality, pornography, and self-gratifying pleasures can be idols, as can material possessions, positions of power and prominence, personal vanity, and the accumulation of wealth for the sake of possessions. Worshipping religion, knowledge, and the institution, ceremony, and the traditions of the church is idolatrous.

Verse 10 reveals a blessed statement: "And he said unto me, Seal not the sayings of the prophecy of this book, for the time is at hand." Revelation is not a secret book; it reveals God's secrets. The Bible contains progressive illumination; throughout the ages, from the first-century church until our twenty-first century, the Holy Spirit has given enlightenment to humanity progressively. The canon of Scripture was closed in AD 95–100, upon the completion of Revelation. The church fathers of the first century examined, studied, compared, and meditated upon the writings of the apostles as inspired by God and issued the first creeds of the church, the foundation of Christian faith and practice according to Scripture.

These are the doctrinal statements of faith we hold fast today: God is self-existent, triune, and the Creator of all things. The Bible is the inspired, inerrant, God-breathed Word. Jesus Christ is the only begotten Son of God, born of the Virgin Mary by the power of the Holy Spirit. Jesus Christ was sinless and without a sin nature and therefore is able and qualified to be our Redeemer. Jesus freely sacrificed His life for all humanity, was buried, and rose bodily on the third day. He ascended to heaven forty days later. The Bible reveals the reality of heaven and hell, salvation and sin, the soon coming and return of Jesus Christ for His church, and the great tribulation to follow. God will accomplish the restoration of Israel as seen in the coming glory of the Second Advent of His Son to His kingdom, from Genesis to the Gospels.

The formation of the early church and the illumination of the book of Acts and the epistle letters of the apostles enlightened Christians in the threefold purpose of the church.

1. To evangelize the lost, share the gospel of Christ, and make disciples of all nations.
2. To edify the saints by preaching and teaching God's Word, by rightly dividing the Word of God, adhering strictly to truth, and obeying the teachings of Christ without compromise.
3. To praise and worship God, give glory and honor to Him, and conform to the image of Jesus Christ.

King Solomon captured it best in Ecclesiastes 12:13: "Let us hear the conclusion of the whole matter, Fear God and keep his commandments, for this is the whole duty of man."

The illumination of the Holy Spirit to the fourteenth-century church on the basis of salvation was proclaimed by Martin Luther's declaration, "*Sola scriptura!*" Scripture alone is final authority, and we are saved by grace alone, by faith alone, by Christ alone, not by works.

The final area of illumination and enlightenment has been given to our generation concerning an area of systematic theology defined as *eschatology, the end-time events according to prophecy.* With this enlightenment, our generation, **the terminal generation,** is without excuse; we can understand the Word of Christ as it relates to our particular generation in these last days. "The time is at hand, and Behold I come quickly."

Verse 11 reveals a final separation in the Bible of the just from the unjust and a warning for the unrighteous and a promise to the redeemed. God has separated the just from the unjust since Creation. God separated the angels of heaven from the unjust that followed Lucifer (Isaiah 14:12–17; Ezekiel 28:1–19; Luke 10:18; Jude 1:5–6; Revelation 12:7–9). God separated Cain from Adam and Eve because he murdered his brother Abel. God separated Noah and his family from the rebellious world in the flood. God separated the young nation of Israel from Pharaoh and Egypt with the first Passover and Exodus from Egypt. God separated the rebellious who worshipped the golden calf of Aaron at the base of Mount Sinai, and God separated Korah and his family and followers in their rebellion against Moses and God's laws in the wilderness. God separated Moses and Aaron and the tribes of

Israel from Miriam, who was Aaron's and Moses' sister when in her pride she attempted to make herself equal to Moses in spiritual authority; God judged her with leprosy. It is a long and exhaustive list.

In His Olivet Discourse, Jesus Christ revealed in the last days of the great tribulation that the unjust world would be separated from the just by the illustration of the nations appearing before Jesus Christ in the separation of the sheep from the goats, the saints from the ungodly. In Matthew 25:41, we read, "Then shall he say unto them on his left hand, depart from me, ye cursed, into everlasting fire, prepared for the devil and his angels."

In verse 11, we are given the description of the just as righteous because they have confessed sin, repented of sin, and accepted Jesus Christ as their personal Savior (Romans 5:1, 8:1). They are holy because they are called the sons of God (Galatians 4:4–7) and because Christ is in them (John 1:11–13).

In verse 11, we are given the description of the unjust as *filthy,* a word not used in many crowd-pleasing sermons today. The best translation of this word is "**to be like dirty earwax.**" The word *filthy* goes to the very heart of an unrepentant sinner—**filthiness of thoughts, imaginations, words, and actions and a blasphemous attitude toward God, the kingdom of God, the Son of God, and the people of God, Jews and Gentiles alike.**

In verses 12 and 13, Jesus Christ declares five things.

1. He will come quickly. It has now been 2,000 years since Revelation was written for our admonition, meditation, and acceptance.
2. His reward is with Him; Jesus Christ will reward all according to their works that will follow them into eternity. These rewards—crowns and reigning assignments—will be given to the faithful at the bema seat of Christ.
3. Jesus declared, "I am the **Alpha and Omega.**"
4. Jesus declared, "I am the **beginning and the end**" (Genesis 1:1; John 1:1; Revelation 22:21).

5. Jesus declared, "I am the **first and the last**." Jesus Christ is the only means of salvation (John 10:13; Acts 4:12; John 3:16–17; 1 John 5:12–13; John 14:6).

The blessings of chapter 22 are in verses 14 and 15: blessed are the saved and the obedient, for they shall have access to the Tree of Life and the city of God. In my years in the ministry, I have heard the regret of many for their poor decisions in life, for yielding to temptation and sin, for wasted opportunities, and for personal failures. I have never heard a Christian lament for having accepted Jesus Christ as his or her personal Savior or say, "I regret getting saved." Salvation is truly joy unspeakable and full of glory!

Notice in this passage the phrase, "for without are dogs?" The word *dog* in Scripture is never used in the sense of a faithful pet. Dogs in Jesus' day were vicious night scavengers. Jezebel was eaten by dogs in the fulfillment of prophecy and God's separation and judgment upon that evil woman. The Syrophenician woman with a daughter possessed by demons used the word *dog* in her plea to Jesus Christ for help in Matthew 15:26. She responded to Jesus that He was correct. "I am a Gentile, but Lord even the dogs eat the crumbs that fall from the Master's Table." Jesus healed her daughter because of her humble plea.

In verses 16 through 19, Jesus gave the last promise, the last warning, and the last prayer in the Bible.

1. Jesus said that He had sent His angel, and this reference best translates as John the apostle as messenger from God with the Words of God and the Revelation testimony about Jesus Christ (Revelation 1–3).
2. Jesus identified Himself as the *root and offspring of David,* recorded in the lineage and genealogy of the Savior. Jesus also identified Himself as the *bright and morning star* (Psalm 19:1).
3. The Holy Spirit call us to Christ, and He calls others through Christians to Christ. The message is always the same: Come and be saved!

4. The last warning of the Bible is "Do not add to the words of this prophecy, and do not take away from the words of this prophecy." The judgment upon this sin is everlasting. God will add the plagues of the judgments upon those who add to the Word of God or pervert or corrupt Scripture with poor Bible translations, interpretations, or insertions of words God did not inspire. God will also remove a name from the Lamb's Book of Life, out of the Holy City, and from those things written in the Bible.

God wrote only one Bible, and that was through human agents inspired by the Holy Ghost. The Bible was written in the two most perfect languages: the Old Testament was written originally in Hebrew, and the New Testament was written in Greek. In these original writings or identical copies abide the infinite perfection that no human will ever duplicate. Between this God-inspired Bible and other writings there exists an impassable gulf over which no member of Adam's race can ever pass and make another book comparable to it. The Word of God is a **unique book** for four reasons.

1. The Bible was **uniquely prepared** through the inspiration of the Holy Ghost moving upon forty men over 1,500 years. The Bible is self-authenticating, inerrant, and in full harmony with itself; it is without contradiction.
2. The Bible is **uniquely preserved.** Throughout history, tyrants, kings, dictators, atheists, and philosophers have attempted the extinction of the Word of God, but the Bible stands as written, and every year is on the *New York Times* list of books outselling all others.
3. The Bible is **unique in its proclamation.** The Bible proclaims that Jesus Christ is the Son of God and the only means and method of salvation.
4. The Bible is **unique in its product. It** is the only book that will produce a Christian (Romans 10:17; 2 Timothy 3:14–15).

God inspired only one Bible; all other writings that are not in full agreement with it cannot possibly be the true Word of God. Two opposing truths cannot occupy the same space. There is but one source of absolute truth (John 8:32, 8:36, 1:14): "I am the way, the truth and the life, and no man comes to the Father but by me."

Several years ago, during a show hosted by David Frost, the archbishop of Canterbury was engaged in a debate with the actress Jane Fonda. The discussion concerned Jesus Christ being the Son of God. Fonda, having been raised in an atheist home, responded to the archbishop that Jesus Christ may be the Son of God to him but not to her. The Archbishop responded, "Dear lady, either Jesus Christ is the Son of God, or He is not. But He cannot be both!" Either the Bible is the inspired and true Word of God or it isn't. The Bible cannot be both, and if the words of Christ are not true, we have been deceived by the worst lie ever foisted on humanity, and of all creatures, we are the most pitiful. But praise to the Lord, God cannot lie.

A multiplicity of differing Bible versions are in circulation today, resulting in a state of bewildering confusion. Some versions (translations that are no longer a word-for-word translation of the original language) omit words, phrases, verses, and even entire portions of text that are well known to have been part of the original manuscripts. In some Bible translations, the Bible has been completely rewritten without regard to proper scriptural exegesis, and the further we stray from what God said, the further we stray from God. The New World Translation of the holy Scriptures from the Watch Tower Bible and Tract Society of Pennsylvania (Jehovah's Witnesses) is a prime example of textual corruption, error, omissions, and word substitutions that satisfy their own personal beliefs apart from what God inspired.

The watering down of the Word of God has been promoted by the marketing phrase of "ease of reading and understanding." These translations of God's Word are no longer word-for-word translations but are now presented as thought-for-thought translations, and in the worst case as a paraphrase of the Bible. God never intended His words to be condensed into a Cliff's Notes or a *Reader's Digest* short story.

Verses 20 and 21 contain the last promise and the last prayer of the Bible. Jesus Christ promised to return quickly, to which John the apostle replied, "Amen! Even so, come quickly, Lord Jesus." For our generation, this promise will be fulfilled quickly, soon, suddenly, and unseen by the world when Jesus Christ calls His bride, the church, away in the rapture, and we will immediately be gathered to be with Christ in the air. There are no remaining prophecies or passages of Scripture or Bible promises to be fulfilled that would prevent the rapture of the church today; it's just that close. We know from our study in the Word of God that Jesus Christ is poised on the horizon of heaven to receive His bride, the church.

Jesus Christ has promised to return bodily in the Second Advent as King of Kings and Lord of Lords, ending the Battle of Armageddon, binding Satan, and judging the anti-Christ, the false prophet, the kings of the earth, and all who worshipped the image of the beast and took his mark, 666. Christ will restore Israel and the faithful remnant as promised in Scripture upon His return.

The final prayer in the Bible is in Revelation 22:21 as a benediction: "**The Grace of our Lord Jesus Christ be with you all. Amen!**" The grace of God is His unmerited favor toward repentant sinners to mercifully forgive our sins and to seal and to save us to His glory through His only begotten Son, Jesus Christ, our Savior.

Most books end with the words "**The End.**" I believe a more appropriate ending would be **"The Beginning!"**

PART IX

THE REVELATION OF JESUS CHRIST FOR THE TERMINAL GENERATION

It was my intent that this study of Revelation would stir the hopes of the discouraged, disheartened, and the confused. Our society is in a dilemma about the economy, political unrest, social disobedience, and the deterioration of the family and home.

Men and women everywhere and from all walks of life are asking the same questions, "What in the world is going on? What will happen next? What will happen to me and my family?" I encourage you to take hope from what you have read and to study and meditate upon the Word of God in Revelation. God is on the throne, in control, and not confused by chaos. The plan of God for the ages is unfolding today before our eyes, and God is bringing this present age to an end.

There is an answer in these difficult last days for our terminal generation, and indeed the circumstances are unparalleled in human history. We are fixed at the crossroads of time and eternity, and the return of Christ rapidly approaches. The answer is in the only begotten Son of God, Jesus Christ. Seek first the kingdom of God and His righteousness. Believe and accept Jesus Christ as your Lord and Savior today. Hold fast to the truths of God's Word, and live one day at a time in the earnest expectation that Christ will carry you all the way.

The Path, Method, and Means of Salvation

"For God so loved the world that he gave his only begotten Son, that whosoever believeth in him should not perish, but have everlasting life" (John 3:16).

"For whosoever shall call upon the name of the Lord shall be saved" (Romans 10:13).

"That if thou shalt confess with thy mouth the Lord Jesus, and shalt believe in thine heart that God hath raised him from the dead, thou shalt be saved. For with the heart man believeth unto righteousness, and with the mouth confession is made unto salvation" (Romans 10:9–10).

The Prayer of Salvation

Father, I ask you now to forgive all my sins and trespasses against you. I believe Jesus died on the cross, was buried, and rose again from the grave, and I accept Jesus Christ as my Savior today. God, help me live for Him as He died for me, amen.

The Assurance of Salvation

"He that hath the son hath life, and he that hath not the son hath not life. These things have I written unto you that believe on the name of the Son of God, that ye may know that ye have eternal life, and that ye may believe on the name of the Son of God" (1 John 5:12–13).

Study Resource Library

Every mature, born-again believer in Jesus Christ should quickly begin to acquire a library of Bible study essentials. The Word of God tells us to "Study to show thyself approved unto God, a workman rightly dividing the word of truth" (2 Timothy 2:15).

Purchase a good study Bible that contains accurate notes from respected theologians in the King James Version, which properly translated from the original languages of the Bible; other translations are incomplete.

Purchase a recommended study Bible: KJV, Moody, Tyndale, Ryrie, Rev. C. I. Schofield, or the Dr. David Jeremiah study Bibles are all excellent selections.

Get *Strong's Exhaustive Concordance of the Bible,* red-letter edition, for original-language word studies, definitions, spelling, and pronunciation.

Also get a good Bible dictionary; Nave's, Smith's, or Harper's are several excellent choices. Purchase a good guide to the Bible such as *Willmington's Guide to the Bible.* A good Bible handbook for quick study references and notes is *The Bible Handbook* by Wilkerson and Boa.

Other good sources are a good, up-to-date Bible atlas for country and city locations and a good, extensive text on systematic theology such as *Systematic Theology* by Wayne Grudem.

Find a Who's Who in the Bible and a commentary on the whole Bible. The late J. V. McGee has an excellent set of five volumes that may be purchased new for less than $100.

Many quality hardbound copies of these books are available used or new online at a fraction of the original cost. You will not regret the investment.

ABOUT THE AUTHOR

Dr. R. C. Courson, Jr., is the son of Robert and Wilma Courson of Danville, Illinois. Dr. Courson graduated from Catlin High School, and went on to complete an associate's degree in liberal studies at his hometown college, DACC, in Danville, Illinois. Dr. Courson also holds a bachelor of science degree from Eastern Illinois University, a bachelor of ministry degree in Bible and evangelism from Crossroads Bible College in Indianapolis, and a master's and a doctorate in theology from Andersonville Theological Seminary in Camilla, Georgia.

Dr. Courson resides in Bedford, Indiana, with his wife, Linda, and has four grown and married children and six grandchildren. He served as a sergeant in the U.S. Marine Corps during the Vietnam War and upon returning home was employed by General Motors Corporation, working there for the next twenty-two years and resigning in 2000 to enter the full-time ministry.

Dr. Courson founded the Last Call Crusade, serving as a nondenominational evangelist proclaiming the Gospels to impoverished neighborhoods and conducting church and tent revivals.

Dr. Courson currently serves as the senior pastor for the First Church of God in Mitchell, Indiana.

—In Christ's service, R. C. Courson Jr., ThD

INFORMATION ABOUT THIS BOOK

Prior to reading and undertaking the study of this book, I encourage you to understand that we are the terminal generation according to empirical, scientific, and biblical evidence that will be presented in this book. Our generation, the baby boomers, the hippies, the yuppies, generation X, and the millennials will be alive when humanity's greatest cataclysmic event sounds in our life.

As you read this book, realize the world and your life as you know it today are about to change forever! Jesus Christ is coming soon, suddenly, and silently to rapture His church, the anti-Christ will ascend to dominate world power, and the wrath of God will be unleashed upon sinful humanity during the great tribulation.

This book is an instruction manual covering the things to come in our life and a survival manual of protection and preparation; be prepared, and don't be left behind!